THE ULTIMATE GUIDE TO THE ★2020★ ELECTION

THE ULTIMATE GUIDE TO THE ★ 2020 ★ ELECTION

101 NONPARTISAN SOLUTIONS TO ALL THE ISSUES THAT MATTER

RYAN CLANCY & MARGARET WHITE
— OF NO LABELS —

DIVERSION
BOOKS

For more information, email info@diversionbooks.com

Diversion Books
A division of Diversion Publishing Corp.
443 Park Avenue South, suite 1004
New York, NY 10016
www.diversionbooks.com

First Diversion Books edition October 2019
Paperback ISBN: 978-1-63576-674-5
eBook ISBN: 978-1-63576-673-8

Printed in The United States of America

3 5 7 9 10 8 6 4 2

Library of Congress cataloging-in-publication data is available on file.

CONTENTS

FOREWORD

Partisanship and polarization aren't new problems in America. But when it really mattered—like in the aftermath of 9/11 or the 2008 financial crisis—Republicans and Democrats in Washington managed to come together to legislate and lead in a way that made America safer and more secure.

We were there, representing Indiana in the Senate and Virginia's 11th District in the House. In the wake of those calamities, we saw real leadership from people on both sides, along with a sense of urgency, clarity, and above all, national unity.

And then it was gone. Soon, the strident partisanship returned, and before long it curdled into something even worse: tribalism, and a growing sense on both sides that one's political opponents were not fellow citizens to be debated but enemies to be destroyed.

This corrosion of our political system and culture was already underway when both of us left Congress about a decade ago. Political scientists can debate the extent to which each side is responsible, but both parties have worked to ratchet up the pressure and widen the divide, needling their adversaries when they were in power, and acting as obstructionists when they were out. Now, with the 2020 election upon us, the tribalism is getting even worse and forcing us to entertain what would have once been an unthinkable question: If another 9/11 or economic crisis hit America tomorrow, could leaders in Washington put aside the petty politics and work with the sense of common purpose and patriotism that has enabled America to endure and thrive through so many dark times throughout our history?

We are not so sure. And that is why we are more committed than we have ever been to the mission of No Labels—where we serve as volunteer advisors—which has been working tirelessly since 2010 to bridge the divide in American politics.

No Labels' mission is difficult but not impossible because this organization speaks for a vast and frustrated majority that is finally waking from its slumber and recognizing the danger that the extremes on both sides pose to America's ability to govern itself. In poll after poll, most Americans say they prefer political leaders willing to compromise to get things done rather than just stick to their principles if it means getting nothing done. And yet, Washington— despite being populated by what many Americans imagine to be weather vanes easily swayed by public opinion—has never seemed more contemptuous of the public's appetite for cooperation.

Why?

The simple answer comes back to something one of us has been saying for years: The partisans have the passion while everyone else has lives.

The fringes on both sides vote, volunteer, show up at the town halls and donate money, and are relentless and disciplined in pushing their message and agenda. They punch well above their weight in political campaigns, especially given the fact that more than eight out of ten US House seats are in districts that are "safe" for one party, which means the primary is the only election that matters. But voter turnout in these races is often between just 10%–20% of the electorate, and most of the people who do turn out are much further to the Left or Right than the country at large.

The Far Left and Far Right may have different ideas, but they are sending the same clear message to political candidates and leaders: "Don't you dare work with the other side. If you do, we are coming for you." That's how we end up with a Congress with too many members who equate compromise with treason and have little interest in forging meaningful working relationships with anyone in the other party.

In Washington and throughout our political system there are plenty of constituencies promoting and profiting from conflict. There has been no constituency for cooperation. But that is starting to change thanks to No Labels, which is finally organizing the vast swath of the public that wants our leaders to work together to solve problems.

Although the easy shorthand explanation for America's dysfunction is the intractable divide between Democrats and Republicans, there is also a growing divide within the parties between their governing and extremist wings. Leaders on the Center Right and Center Left are finding they may have more in common with one another than the fringes in their own parties, and with that recognition comes the potential for a welcome and overdue realignment in American politics.

Thus far in the 2020 election, neither President Trump nor the many Democrats vying to replace him appear interested in speaking to voters beyond their base. But as we approach next year's election—and the candidates recognize the coalition necessary to win a party primary is very different from the one required to win a general—they'll have to move beyond narrowcasting to their base and toward broadcasting to the country. When they do, they and their campaigns would be well-served to read the book Ryan Clancy and Margaret White have written.

No Labels' *Ultimate Guide to the 2020 Election* cuts through the noise and the partisan spin to explain the nature of America's problems and the policy choices available to the next president. In a political environment in which each side wants to make every issue seem black and white, Margaret and Ryan will help you understand the many shades of gray. After you read this book, we think you'll recognize that Americans aren't as hopelessly divided as some imagine.

There is common ground to be found, if only our leaders are willing to look for it.

We don't agree with every single idea Margaret and Ryan propose in the *Ultimate Guide*. But we are proud to write the foreword for this book because we believe Margaret and Ryan have approached our nation's challenges in much the same way we tried to throughout our careers in Congress: identifying a problem, researching several ideas across the ideological spectrum for how to fix it, and proposing solutions that they believe could generate broad bipartisan support.

That approach has not only produced a book worth reading; it offers a blueprint for how our next president could unite the country and bring both parties together to solve problems that have festered for far too long.

We aren't naïve about how hard this will be. The incentives for politicians on both sides to pander to their base and try to destroy the other side are as strong as they have ever been. But there is another way forward, and No Labels' *Ultimate Guide to the 2020 Election* points the way.

Evan Bayh and Tom Davis, May 2019

Tom Davis, a Republican, represented Virginia's 11th district in the US House from 1995–2008. He also chaired the National Republican Congressional Committee from 1999–2003.

Evan Bayh, a Democrat, was the governor of Indiana from 1989–1997 and served as a US Senator from 1999–2011.

★ INTRODUCTION ★

A NATION DIVIDED

or years, we've worked together as leaders of No Labels, a national organization of Democrats, Republicans, and independents trying to bring America's political leaders together to solve problems.

We know this idea sounds crazy in 2019. Democrats and Republicans don't appear to agree on much of anything, and "hate" does not seem too strong a word for how many partisans feel about the other side.

This goes well beyond the familiar polarization and legislative gridlock people complained about when No Labels launched in 2010. What's happening in American politics lately is new, different, and scary: Reason and persuasion—the pillars of our democracy since its founding—are out. Anger and intimidation are in.

As the 2020 presidential election shapes up, it doesn't feel like a battle of ideas so much as a war of two tribes bent on the other's destruction. President Trump says his opponents hate America, and he appears poised to spend the next year firing up his base with endless tweet storms trolling Hollywood, the elites, globalists, and the Left. Meanwhile, the progressive base—fueled by seething hatred for Trump—pushes Democratic primary contenders to embrace the most left-wing policy agenda in generations. We seem headed for a depressing and dispiriting slog to November 2020, when one candidate manages to convince a bare majority of Americans that they are not as bad as their opponent.

But what if the American people demanded something different?

Though the extremes seem to dominate our national conversation, they don't represent anything close to a majority of Americans. A 2018 study by the group More in Common classified just 14% of Americans as "Devoted Conservatives" or "Progressive Activists." Stuck in between are the two-thirds of Americans who belong to an "exhausted majority," united by their "sense of fatigue with our polarized national conversation, a willingness to be flexible in their political viewpoints, and a lack of voice in the national conversation."

No Labels' *Ultimate Guide to the 2020 Election* aims to give a voice to this exhausted majority, to provide an unbiased look at the challenges facing America, and to outline the shape of a new agenda that we believe can unite our divided country.

THE ULTIMATE GUIDE TO THE ★ 2020 ★ ELECTION

A ROADMAP FOR UNITY 2020

★ 1 ★

OUR DISRUPTED DEMOCRACY

Since **1939, Gallup** pollsters have been asking the American public to identify the biggest problem facing our country. In the February 2019 poll, 35% named government, poor leadership, or politicians as the single greatest problem facing the US—the highest percentage who made this choice in at least 55 years.

How did it get this bad, this fast?

We blame the iPhone.

No, Apple is not to blame for upending American democracy. But technology is. In the last 30 years, technology has radically reshaped every aspect of our lives—how we work, how we play, and how we connect to one another. But our political system has barely changed at all. And it simply can't keep up.

Our political system is still stuck in the Industrial Age, and it has no way to deal with the changes brought about by the Information Age. And neither do many of the citizens and communities across the country—and around the world—who increasingly feel left behind.

It only gets harder from here because technology doesn't progress in a linear fashion. It progresses exponentially.

In 1965, Gordon Moore—the founder of Intel, which invented the first microprocessor—made a prescient prediction. He said the number of transistors you could fit on an integrated circuit—a measure of the amount of processing power you could pack into a chip—would double every two years. Moore's Law, as it became known, held true for over 50 years, and it explains why your smartphone has more computing power than all of NASA possessed in 1969 when it sent a man to the moon.

Technology unquestionably makes our lives better. Thanks to technology and innovation, we have conquered diseases, saved lives, developed cleaner energy, and created unprecedented prosperity. Life is more convenient than many of us ever imagined.

But technology always brings disruption. It was true when millions moved from farms to factories at the turn of the 20th century. It's still true today.

Technology has usually followed a familiar pattern: When breakthrough innovations happen—like the advent of the cotton gin, the steam engine, the car, or the internet—they kill old, unproductive industries and jobs. And they create new and better ones.

When this change happens over decades, communities and our political system have time to adjust. But today, this change is happening instantaneously. And our political system isn't remotely equipped to handle it.

You could argue that Donald Trump is the 45th president of the United States because he told Americans a simple story: "You are worse off—and good jobs are harder to find—because of immigration and bad trade deals."

Most who've researched the issue don't endorse the president's view, with one notable study finding that 85% of lost US manufacturing jobs resulted from technological change, not trade. The real problem isn't NAFTA. It's the factory that used to employ 10,000 people but now employs 1,000 with robots doing the rest. A 2019 Brookings Institution report found that as many as a quarter of the current jobs in the US are at risk of being disrupted by artificial intelligence (AI).

Just look at truck driving, which is the most common occupation in 29 states and provides a solid middle-class income. In 2015, the first self-driving semitruck was tested in Nevada. Uber has started testing driverless cars on public roads.

So let's do a little thought experiment together. If AI decimates the top job in most states, what do you think will happen to our already fragile democracy?

Answer: It will strain it like never before, unless we do something about it.

Knowing this is coming, as many politicians in Washington do, you would imagine that the future and the challenges of technological change would be front and center in our political debate. But in their own way, both the Left and Right are pushing agendas rooted in the distant past.

☆ WHAT DO WE MEAN BY ☆ "RIGHT" AND "LEFT"?

The 2020 presidential race has featured almost two dozen candidates running. In this book, we will explain the kinds of policies the Left and the Right are pushing these candidates to embrace. It is important, however, to first define the "Left" and "Right." Although the Left does include radicals like Antifa and the Right includes white nationalists, these groups aren't our focus. For the purposes of this book, when we mention "Left" and "Right," we invite you to think of the most ideological flanks of the Congressional Progressive Caucus and the Freedom Caucus. It's still a rough proxy, but we hope you get the point.

THE GREEN NEW DEAL VS MAKE AMERICA GREAT AGAIN

The Green New Deal, proposed in early 2019 by Rep. Alexandria Ocasio-Cortez (D-NY) and Sen. Edward Markey (D-MA) and endorsed by several Democratic presidential contenders, is still more aspirational idea than actual policy agenda. But it envisions a "new national, social, industrial, and economic mobilization on a scale not seen since World War II" to combat climate change, to correct economic and social injustices, and to guarantee employment, housing, and health care.

Make America Great Again combines a mix of 1950s nostalgia, 1980s economics, and President Trump's skepticism toward trade and immigration.

The Green New Deal and Make America Great Again resonate because they speak to real and urgent concerns. Climate change is happening, and it's getting worse. Globalization and free trade have not distributed their benefits equitably, and too many American communities have been left behind with little hope for the future.

Meanwhile, business and political leaders have contributed to or overseen catastrophic failures like the 2008 financial crisis while others suffered the consequences. No one went to jail. No one took the blame. They got reelected. They got bonuses. Millions of Americans, on the other hand, lost their jobs and were evicted from their homes.

Americans are ticked off, and they have a right to be.

Make America Great Again and the Green New Deal offer radically different visions to address this anger. But they both tap into a deep well of anger in the electorate, and they are great brands. Trump, of course, rode Make America Great Again to victory in 2016. As of early 2019, large majorities of Americans said they supported the goals of the Green New Deal. The problem—as we'll explore throughout this book—is that both visions too often entail simplistic, unworkable solutions to exceptionally complex challenges.

Make America Great Again and the Green New Deal—when you look behind the slogans and into the policies—are underpinned by several ideas that push the country much further Right or Left than most Americans want to go.

This is a feature, not a bug. The way incentives are set up in our system today, politicians and even presidential candidates don't need to care about what the majority wants. They only need to respond to the comparatively small number of people and interest groups who fund their campaigns and turn out to vote for them in elections—especially the primary elections that narrow Americans' choices more than most of us appreciate.

Partisans on the Left and the Right increasingly subscribe to what we at No Labels have long called the "king (or queen) for a day delusion." It goes a little something like this: *If we just fight long and hard enough for what we believe in, we will prevail. We will win enough power in some future election to ram through every item on our wish list. And we won't have to deal with those evil people on the other side.*

But that day never comes. In a divided country, neither party can ever get all the power it wants. In the instances when one party fully controls the White House and Congress—as when Democrats unilaterally passed the Affordable Care Act in 2010 with no Republican votes and Republicans passed the Tax Cuts and Jobs Act in 2017 with no Democratic votes—the opposing party immediately tries to dismantle what was just passed. Instead of recognizing the folly of this approach, the extreme partisans double down, demanding more purity and less flexibility in a vicious cycle that never ends. And we end up where we are now, where no one is happy with the status quo, everyone is angry, and our country's problems keep getting worse.

As we write this, virtually every force in US politics—money, votes, grassroots energy, and enthusiasm—is pushing our political leaders and parties in one direction: apart.

The only viable answer to these radical forces dividing America is to create equally strong forces pushing in the other direction.

NO LABELS: BRIDGING THE DIVIDE

No Labels was launched in 2010 as an effort to answer two pressing questions about American politics:

- Is there a way to bridge the growing chasm separating the two parties?
- Could an outside group create incentives to prompt the nation's political leaders to put country above party?

Judging from the daily headlines about Washington's dysfunction almost a decade later, you could be forgiven for thinking the answer to both these questions is an unequivocal "No." But No Labels has quietly and consistently built a formidable infrastructure of allies in Congress, ideas, and citizens working to create a space in the political center where solutions can be forged.

Congress

No Labels spent years just trying to get members of Congress from both parties into a room together. Early on, one of us was meeting with a member of Congress in his office when he pointed across the hallway to the office of a three-term member of the other party and said, "I have never really had a conversation with him before."

It was a clarifying moment in which we realized just how dysfunctional our government had become. After all, how could these members possibly work together to solve tough issues if they didn't like, trust, or even know one another?

It wasn't easy, but over time, these meetings built trust, led to legislation, and ultimately to something that had never before existed on Capitol Hill: the creation of a durable bipartisan bloc committed to getting to "yes" on key issues. It's called the Problem Solvers Caucus.

In the 2017–2018 session of Congress, the Problem Solvers—which has over 40 members—developed their own bylaws and standards of behavior designed to give them the same sort of voice groups like the Freedom Caucus and Progressive Caucus claimed by sticking together. After long, arduous nights of negotiation, the Problem Solvers emerged publicly with the only bipartisan fix for health care and then a range of bipartisan solutions on gun safety, infrastructure, and immigration and border security. You probably never heard about most of these efforts because House rules and leaders prevented the Problem Solvers' bipartisan bills from even getting a vote.

Encouraged by the Problem Solvers Caucus's ability to come together on tough issues, but frustrated by the refusal of House leadership to seriously consider these proposals, No Labels, in June 2018, announced *The Speaker Project*, a reform plan that proposed using the election of a new Speaker of the House as leverage to make rules changes that would give bipartisan ideas a fair hearing and a fighting chance in the next Congress. On July 25, the Problem Solvers Caucus released *Break the Gridlock*, which had the same goals and echoed many of the same proposals originally offered in *The Speaker Project*. Twenty Caucus members later committed to only vote for a House Speaker who supported these rule reforms.

On November 28, nine Democratic members of the House Problem Solvers Caucus announced they had reached agreement with Speaker Nancy Pelosi and Democratic leadership on an ambitious rules reform package that made it easier for bipartisan legislation to get a fair hearing in this Congress. Notably, three Republican members of the Problem Solvers Caucus crossed over to vote for the

Democratic rules package—the first time that has happened in two decades.

This amounted to the most significant House rules changes in decades and the *Washington Post* praised No Labels and the Problem Solvers for taking the "heat" required to make it happen.

The Problems Solvers Caucus is an independent, member-driven organization—which means it is separate from No Labels and sets its own agenda and develops its own policy positions—but No Labels believes the existence of the Caucus proves that a bipartisan bloc can thrive in this era of polarized politics.

Ideas

No Labels regularly releases reform proposals and books—often informed by in-depth public opinion research—to constructively shape the policy debate. These include:

- *The 2016 Policy Playbook for America's Next President*
- Procedural and process reform plans focused on various areas of the federal government (*Make Congress Work!, Make the Presidency Work!, Make Government Work!*)
- Books, including *No Labels: A Shared Vision for a Stronger America; Just the Facts;* and *How? No Labels Answers the Most Important Question of the 2016 Election*

Some of the ideas introduced in these books went on to become law, most notably "No Budget, No Pay," which was premised on the simple idea that members of Congress shouldn't be paid if they don't pass a budget on time. The idea was implemented as part of a 2013 budget deal, and No Labels continues today to push for its permanent adoption.

Citizens

No Labels is a citizen-fueled movement that counts over one million supporters across the country who believe the defining challenges of our time can only be solved with support from both of our political parties.

Most days, members of Congress are inundated with calls and emails from the angriest and most intransigent voices back home, almost always telling them to say "no" to something. Our citizens are helping leaders in Congress understand there is a numerically larger and passionate group of citizens who will show up at town halls, call and write congressional offices, and support members who are willing to reach across the aisle. With an active presence online, and in local communities, No Labels depends on its citizens to recruit new members and to mobilize at key moments to persuade elected officials to embrace common-sense bipartisan legislation.

LOOKING AHEAD

No Labels is creating a new center of gravity in American politics in which the forces in our system align to encourage politicians to come together to solve problems. Our work is quietly paying dividends as No Labels counts over a million supporters online and has citizen-led chapters in every state.

Cynics often write off groups like No Labels as squishy centrists or mushy moderates—the kind of people who beg politicians to be nice to one another and settle for a lowest common denominator compromise between the two parties.

That's not what this is about.

We know that there are real philosophical differences between Democrats and Republicans that can't be papered over with nice words about civility and cooperation. But we also know that throughout history, having Democrats and Republicans at the table and invested in the success of legislation has delivered the most consequential and durable reforms. These include: the creation of Social Security in the 1930s, the passage of Medicare and the Civil Rights Act in the 1960s, tax reform in the 1980s, and the balancing of the budget in the 1990s.

Even amid Washington's dysfunction in 2018, Congress passed and the president signed bipartisan legislation to fight opioid abuse, reform financial regulatory laws, and deliver the most significant criminal justice reforms in decades.

But finding this common ground requires a certain kind of attitude—one that is increasingly dismissed by the Left and Right. It requires a willingness to sit down with anyone—conservative, liberal, or somewhere in between—so long as they are willing to work together to find solutions. It means recognizing that having principled and deeply held political beliefs doesn't require an all-or-nothing approach to governance. In fact, this attitude is what created this mess in the first place. It's too often the dominant attitude on the 2020 campaign trail, and it needs to change.

And this is why we decided to write No Labels' *Ultimate Guide to the 2020 Election.*

★ 3 ★

THE 2020 UNITY AGENDA

The late Sen. Daniel Patrick Moynihan (D-NY) famously said, "Everyone is entitled to his own opinion, but not his own facts."

But even a casual observer of American politics knows that everyone now has their own facts. The people who watch *Fox News* live in one reality. Those who watch *MSNBC* live in another. Without any agreement on where the country actually is, it's proving impossible to get agreement on where we need to go.

The first thing we hope to do with the *Ultimate Guide* is to build a foundation of facts to help citizens understand the shape and causes of our toughest problems.

- ◆ Why is health care so expensive?
- ◆ Why is our immigration system so broken?
- ◆ Why is the political system so dysfunctional?
- ◆ What can be done about the size and influence of huge tech companies?
- ◆ Does the American Dream still exist?
- ◆ Is there any way to bridge the partisan divide on climate change?

We hope you'll find answers to these questions and others throughout the course of this book.

Throughout each of our policy chapters, we've also provided sample questions that citizens and members of the media can—and will, we hope—ask of President Trump and the Democratic candidates when they appear at political events in communities across the country.

Finally, we aim to help you understand the choices available to deal with our problems. We explain what is being offered by the Right and Left. And we present our own ideas that we collectively call the 2020 Unity Agenda.

The solutions offered in the 2020 Unity Agenda are underpinned by two core values:

- *Opportunity* means that all Americans should be able to go as far as their gifts and drive can take them, and that government policy should encourage and cultivate these gifts.
- *Mutual Responsibility* means that both citizens and the government owe something to one another. If citizens work hard and engage in our democracy and civic life, they have a right to expect a government that will solve the problems too large and systemic for citizens or private actors to solve alone. They also expect the government to help catch those Americans who fall through the cracks, whether because of luck, circumstance, or systemic injustice.

Our ambition for the *Ultimate Guide* is not to fuel an independent bid for president. And given the strong pull of partisans, we don't expect Donald Trump to suddenly abandon Make America Great Again nor for Democrats to turn on the Green New Deal. Instead, our aim is to help Americans understand the real challenges that we face and to see that they have a broader set of choices—of leaders and of policy—than they are currently being offered.

If any of the presidential candidates want to reach beyond their base to speak to the massive but massively unrepresented "exhausted majority," we think they could do a lot worse than embracing the ideas offered in our Unity Agenda.

☆ **THE NEW CENTER** ☆

Many of the ideas in this book came from a new nonprofit called The New Center, whose mission is to "establish the intellectual basis for a viable political center in today's America." This book would not be possible without the hard work of The New Center's policy analysts: Julia Baumel, Evan Burke, Zane Heflin, Laurin Schwab, and Aleksandra Srdanovic. We owe them a huge debt of gratitude.

In the chapters ahead you'll find various policy solutions to America's pressing challenges, but for those who want to dig deeper into policy, The New Center will also release companion papers throughout 2019 and 2020 at www.newcenter.org, that provide more context and granularity surrounding many of these solutions.

POLICY OUTLINE

Our 2020 Unity Agenda doesn't address every problem. But it tackles many of the biggest ones that will be front and center in the presidential campaign, including:

- Health care
- Energy and climate change
- Infrastructure
- The rise of "Big Tech"
- The American Dream
- Immigration
- The "Magic Money Tree" (i.e., the national debt)
- Gun safety

Our final—and perhaps most important—policy ideas address the "System," with ideas that could revitalize our campaign process and restore our democracy.

Here is a brief overview of our 2020 Unity Agenda:

Health Care for All

One hundred eighty-one million Americans get health care insurance through their jobs. Most are happy with it. Instead of blowing up the current health care system, fix the parts that don't work. Below are solutions for expanding health care access and coverage, reducing costs, addressing the opioid epidemic, and reducing medical errors:

- *Address the Doctor Shortage* with more medical schools, more foreign doctors, and by empowering nurses and nurse practitioners to deliver more care.
- *Lower Medicare Buy-In Age From 65 to 55.*
- *A Public Option*: Create a federally administered public health insurance plan that would be eligible to anyone currently enrolled in Medicaid or an insurance plan through one of the Affordable Care Act exchanges.
- *Catastrophic Care for All*: Enroll every American in a high-deductible health care plan that pays for basic preventive care and provides coverage for the catastrophic expenses, like accidents and serious diseases, that drive too many families to bankruptcy.
- *Let the States Innovate* with the individual health insurance exchanges. (Unleash the laboratories of democracy!)
- *Change How Medicaid and Medicare Pay*: Value over volume.
- *Let Medicare Negotiate Drug Prices.* (The VA does it. Why can't Medicare?)
- *Real Price Transparency*: Empower consumers to shop for the most affordable care.
- *Stop the Crazy Lawsuits*: Implement real tort reform to prevent the "defensive medicine" that costs over $100 million per year.
- *Curb the Influence of Drug Industry Middlemen*: Pharmacy benefit managers may be jacking up the price you pay for medicine.
- *Don't Let Companies Game the Patent System*: Curb the costs

of the biologic medicines that account for 40% of all prescription drug spending in the US.

- *Answer the End-of-Life Question* with an Advance Directive for everyone who signs up for Medicare.
- *An Alzheimer's Moon Shot*: Significantly increase funding to fight a disease that could cost us $1 trillion per year by mid-century.
- *Treat Addicts Like Patients, Not Criminals*: Only one in five addicts get the care they need.
- *Real Data Interoperability*: Standardize electronic medical records.

Energy Innovation

The Right wants to ignore climate change. The Left wants to radically disrupt virtually every part of America's economy and society to fight it. Neither approach makes sense. The only way to solve the problem is with breakthrough energy technologies that provide the same thing that fossil fuels do: cheap, abundant, and affordable power on a massive scale.

- *Double Down on Federal R&D*: Breakthrough energy technologies—including the fracking technology that made the US the Saudi Arabia of natural gas—often spring from government research labs or from government grants for basic R&D.
- *Put a Price on Carbon…and Put the Money in People's Pockets*: Put a steadily rising fee on fossil fuels with dividends rebated directly back to US households each month (sometimes called "carbon fee and dividend").

Infrastructure: Real Funding and Real Flexibility

American infrastructure is terrible thanks to decades of underinvestment (we should be spending $200B more per year) and red tape that makes it too hard to start and finish projects (projects that take two years to finish in Europe take eight years in the US).

- *Funding Ideas*: More user fees like a freight tax; public-private partnerships; interstate highways tolls; one point increase in corporate income tax; more institutional (e.g., pension fund) investment; open up infrastructure investments to individuals.
- *Less Red Tape*: Make federal infrastructure funding contingent on local permitting reforms; give states more flexibility to spend on priority projects.
- *A Better Process for Prioritizing Investments* judged on how they enhance public safety or improve the economy.
- *A Capital Budget*: Congress needs one so that the economic return of infrastructure investments is considered along with the cost for budget scoring purposes.

Take on Big Tech

Big tech companies know everything about us, and they are bigger and more powerful than any companies in history. They're exemplars of American innovation, but they have also crossed a line that violates our privacy and threatens fair competition in our economy.

- *Congress Needs to Get Smart on Tech* by bringing back the Office of Technology Assessment.
- *Protect People's Privacy* with federal legislation that gives consumers more control over their personal data.
- *Ethical Standards for Artificial Intelligence* to ensure there are guardrails around what AI can and can't do as it is able to assume more roles and responsibilities in the years ahead.
- *Real Transparency*: Industry should create common standards to establish a clear process for reviewing and removing material from online platforms.
- *Approach "Safe Harbor" with Caution*: It may be time to revisit the 1996 law protecting early internet companies from litigation over content on their platforms, but unintended consequences could harm smaller companies.
- *Better Laws to Promote Competition*: The major US laws gov-

erning competition—such as the Sherman Act of 1890—
were passed over a century ago. Time for a refresh.

* *Better Enforcement*: It's been over 20 years since the Justice
  Department took on Microsoft for its anticompetitive practices. No case of similar impact has been brought since.

The New American Dream

Is the American Dream still alive? It depends whom you ask. The
next president should support policies that support the many features that are working in the US economy but with a much more
targeted focus on Americans who are unquestionably being left behind. Here are a few ideas for leveling the playing field:

* *Make Work Pay*: Motivate potential workers to join the workforce by expanding the earned income tax credit, wage subsidy pilots, and reforms to disability and unemployment
  insurance.
* *Train the Workforce of the Future*: Displaced workers need
  more help finding work in different industries via a new
  training tax credit, federal financial aid for career education, and by targeting that aid to the low- and middle-income students who need it most.
* *Help Working Families*: One in five American families spends
  more than a quarter of their income on childcare. Ideas to
  ease the burden include subsidized family leave and an expanded childcare tax credit.
* *Help Americans Go to Where the Jobs Are* by expanding the
  availability of financial support for individuals who want to
  make long-distance moves to places promising greater economic opportunity.
* *Ease the College Debt Burden* with longer loan repayment
  terms tied to income.
* *Make Colleges More Accountable for Reducing Costs*: Colleges
  that don't keep tuition increases under cost of inflation would
  risk having students lose access to federal student loans.

- ◆ *Incentivize College Completion* by giving more aid to schools that help students finish rather than just start school.
- ◆ *Give Workers a Fair Share* by incentivizing companies to implement more profit-sharing plans.
- ◆ *Close the Skills Gap*: Provide universal computer science education, more targeted STEM investments in middle and high schoolers, and new avenues for worker accreditation. Make more educational funding conditioned upon students pursuing majors in areas where there are projected future job shortages.
- ◆ *A Second Chance to Get Ahead*: More education and job training for the previously incarcerated.
- ◆ *Boost Small Businesses* with a regulatory roadmap for entrepreneurs and expansions of the Community Reinvestment Act and the Rural Business Investment Program.

Immigration: High Wall, Big Gate

America's immigration system has not been comprehensively reformed since 1965. The following grand bargain could meet both the policy and political imperatives of the current moment.

- ◆ *Shift Toward More Employment-Based Immigration*: The US currently admits almost five times as many immigrants for family-based reasons as employment-related ones. We should shift our targets closer to those from countries like Canada, which has an almost equal split.
- ◆ *Get the Undocumented Out of the Shadows*: The 11 million unauthorized immigrants living in the US should be offered a long and rigorous road toward citizenship.
- ◆ *Build a Wall Where It Works*: It is essential to have a fortified border—with fencing, walls, and natural barriers—that allows the US to reliably and consistently prevent unauthorized entry.
- ◆ *Internal Immigration Enforcement and Detention*: There are more illegal immigrants who came to the US legally but became illegal by overstaying their visas than there are un-

authorized border crossers. Employers need to take the lead on visa overstays with E-Verify, and ICE needs to clean up the abuse in its internal detention system by banning private prisons.

- *Address the Source of the Asylum Problem*: Don't reduce aid to troubled Latin and Central American countries. Increase it.
- *Let the Kids Stay*: On average, Dreamers were brought to the US by their parents when they were six years old, and 97% of them are working or in school.

The Magic Money Tree: A Real Plan

This phrase aptly describes how both Democratic and Republican presidential candidates apparently plan to pay for their promises and reduce our massive national debt. In short, they don't have a plan. Dealing with the debt requires Congress and the president to come to the table even if they don't want to.

- *A Fiscal Responsibility Act*: This would implement a new public debt/GDP limit that could only be violated with a formal Declaration of War or a supermajority vote of both houses of Congress and the signature of the president.
- *No Budget, No Pay*: If Congress can't make spending and budget decisions on time, its members should not get paid.
- *Biennial Budgeting*: Congress should establish a two-year "biennial" budgeting cycle for the US government, which would enable members to focus more on long-term strategic planning.
- *Annual Fiscal Report*: Every year, a nonpartisan leader such as the comptroller general should deliver a televised fiscal update in person to a joint session of Congress.

Gun Safety

Almost 40,000 Americans were killed by guns in 2017, the highest level in nearly 40 years. No other developed country comes close. The next president must lead a different conversation on guns—

one that respects the rights and views of law-abiding gun owners, is grounded in facts instead of emotion, and ultimately leads to reforms that diminish the unconscionable toll that gun violence has on American society. Here are some ideas:

- *Extreme Risk Protection Orders* to make it easier for guns to be temporarily taken from people that family, friends, or law enforcement deem to be a risk to themselves or others.
- *Crack Down on Irresponsible Gun Dealers*: 1% of gun dealers are responsible for 60% of the guns found at crime scenes.
- *Raise the Gun-Buying Age to 21*: Congress is considering upping the age to buy tobacco to 21. Why not guns?
- *Universal Background Checks*: 22% of all weapons are purchased without a background check.
- *More Gun Violence Research*: Restrictions on federal research means we don't know nearly enough about the causes of—and solutions to—gun violence.
- *Look to the States*: Many states—including ones led by Republican governors and legislators—have recently passed laws to keep guns away from dangerous people. Washington should take note.
- *A "Grand Bargain" on Guns*: If the next president wants to go big, propose the creation of one federally issued license for possession of all semiautomatic firearms. The gun control side gives up the possibility of a federal gun registry, specific states abandon their weapon bans and long gun registries, and, in exchange, the gun rights side accepts a brand-new federal licensing scheme with real teeth.

Fixing the System: More Conversation, Less Gridlock

Our political system—the process through which we elect our leaders, and the rules they labor under once they get elected—is broken. That means that even if America is lucky enough to see a perfect storm in which we elect good leaders with good ideas, we can still get bad results. Here are a few big ideas to reform American politics.

- ◆ *National Primary Day* to boost turnout across the political spectrum: Primary elections are every bit as—if not more— important as general elections, but turnout is low and dominated by extremists on both sides.
- ◆ *End the Supreme Court Circus* by eliminating lifetime appointments to the court and having justices serve one 18-year term.
- ◆ *Universal National Service*: Require young people to devote one year of their lives to national service. It wouldn't be a panacea, but in bringing together Americans—of different creeds, backgrounds, and political beliefs—to solve problems, it would remind us that what unites us as Americans is so much greater than what divides us.
- ◆ *Revive Civic Education*: Just 26% of Americans can name all three branches of government.
- ◆ *Regular Presidential News Conferences and Question Time*: A way to break through the spin, speeches, and tweets to force presidents to answer tough questions about pressing issues and to be accountable to the voters who put them in office.
- ◆ *Regular Bipartisan Meetings*: Fewer partisan pep rallies. More bipartisan discussions about solutions.
- ◆ *Fix (But Don't Dump) the Filibuster*: Curb the obstruction and gridlock while protecting minority party rights.
- ◆ *Bring Back Earmarks*: Critics call it "pork barrel spending." We call it necessary for Congress to get things done.

This is just a brief outline of an agenda that speaks to the vast exhausted majority of Americans who demand something better from our politics. The following chapters illuminate our positions in much more detail, using facts and polls to explain precisely why many of the solutions from the Left and Right fall short of achieving our collective policy goals on all the issues that matter. Additionally, the "2020 Candidate Questions" provide actionable tools that all US voters can use to hold our politicians accountable and push them to articulate unifying policies that will solve our toughest problems.

In closing, we want to emphasize that any policy platform is only as strong as the grassroots support behind it. So if you like the shape of the Unity Agenda and want more information on how you can push it and the No Labels movement forward, please visit www.no-labels.org/jointhemovement.

CONFRONTING THE CONFIDENCE CRISIS

Each month for decades, Gallup has been asking Americans if they are "satisfied with the way things are going in the United States."

The "satisfied" number hasn't cleared 40% in almost fourteen years.

America is mired in a long-running confidence crisis.

We have way too much of one kind of confidence and far too little of another. Unfortunately, the one we have too little of is the one we need to get our country moving again.

The confidence held by too many on the Right and Left is that they and only they know what is wrong with our country and how to fix it. It is the confidence that people with different views aren't just wrong but stupid, evil, or treasonous.

As this pernicious kind of confidence has risen, the other absolutely essential American confidence has evaporated: The confidence that tomorrow will be just a little better than yesterday.

It may sound trite, but this confidence is the secret sauce of America's centuries-long success story.

With confidence, a people and a country can take risks to build a brighter future. With confidence, our decisions are driven by potential and opportunity instead of fear.

We will rediscover this confidence only when our political leaders—and our president—commit to the cause of national unity as a national imperative.

We hope this book gives the American people the knowledge and the tools to push the 2020 contenders to unite the country rather than divide it.

PART

THE ISSUES

★ 4 ★
HEALTH CARE

n 2010, Congress passed and President Obama signed into law the Affordable Care Act, arguably the most significant health care reform since the advent of Medicare and Medicaid in 1965. Even as the law expanded coverage to tens of millions of people and implemented welcome reforms, like prohibiting insurance companies from discriminating against people with pre-existing conditions, it was unwieldy with plenty of unintended consequences.

In short, much still needs fixing in American health care. While the system can deliver world-class care, access to that care is still uneven. And though America leads the world in its development of medical breakthroughs, the resulting treatments are often prohibitively expensive.

For the better part of a decade, the health care "debate" in America has been singularly defined by the Affordable Care Act, with its detractors doing little more than trying to tear it down without offering much of a counter-solution. It is time for the health care debate to move on and for the next president to continue the work to make American health care more accessible and affordable.

American health care is defined by two problems that desperately need fixing:

PROBLEM #1:
HEALTH CARE IS WAY TOO EXPENSIVE

+ $15 for a single Tylenol pill. $10 for the little paper cup that holds the pill. $53 for a pair of latex gloves. $800 for a sterile water IV bag. These are actual costs that appeared on actual bills of patients in US hospitals.

+ The average American knee replacement costs as much as a Tesla.

+ As a share of its economy, the US spends about twice as much as other developed countries with worse outcomes for critical measures like life expectancy and infant mortality.

+ Family health insurance premiums are growing twice as fast as workers' earnings.

What's causing it?

+ *No One Knows What Anything Costs*: In a 2017 survey, three of four US adults said they didn't know of a resource to help them compare costs among providers.

+ *Drug Prices Are Obscene*: Americans pay three times more than the British for the same prescription drugs.

+ *Admin Overload*: American doctors spend twice as much time filling out paperwork as seeing patients.

+ *End-of-Life Care*: One out of every four Medicare dollars— over $125 billion annually—is spent on care near the end of life, much of which may be unnecessary, unwanted by patients or their family, and adds little to the quality or length of a person's life.

+ *"Defensive Medicine"*: Several studies suggest that medical malpractice suits and defensive medicine—the practice of doctors ordering unnecessary tests and treatments to protect against litigation—cost an excess of $100 billion each year.

HEALTH CARE

Relative contributions to total national health expenditures, 2017

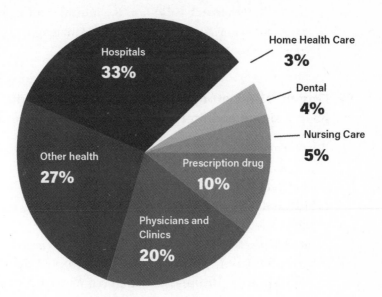

Source: Kaiser Family Foundation analysis of National Health Expenditure (NHE) Data

PROBLEM #2:
TOO MANY PEOPLE ARE DYING NEEDLESSLY

Here are some horrifying statistics that help explain why:

1. Medical errors are the third-leading cause of death in the US after heart disease and cancer.

What's causing it?

- *Unreliable Patient Information*: A 2018 study found that 85.5% of patients lost or gained a diagnosis when their medical records were transferred between hospitals.
- *Incompatible Information Systems*: In 2015, fewer than one in three American hospitals was able to find, send, receive, and integrate electronic information from outside providers.

* *Uneven Safety Standards*: In 2006, California founded a state-wide maternal mortality care collaborative that lowered the state's maternal death rate by more than half between 2006 and 2013. Other states did not. Excluding California and Texas, the maternal death rate in the US increased by 26.6% from 2000 to 2014.

2. Fifty-four percent of rural American counties did not have a single hospital with obstetric services in 2017.

What's causing it?

* *Hospital Closures*: Sixty-four rural hospitals closed between 2013 and 2017, which is more than twice as many closures as the previous five-year period.
* *Too Few Doctors*: In 2014, a fifth of Americans lived in rural areas, but barely a tenth of physicians worked there. The National Rural Health Association estimates that there are almost nine times more specialists in urban areas than rural ones.
* *Rural Hospitals Can't Turn a Profit*: About 60% of rural hospitals' revenues come from Medicaid and Medicare compared to 45% of urban hospitals' revenues. Some states, however, chose not to expand Medicaid after passage of the Affordable Care Act, and rural hospitals closed more in these states than others.

3. More Americans died by drug overdose in 2017 than the number of American servicemen killed during the entire Vietnam War.

What's causing it?

* *Not Enough Treatment*: Fewer than one in five people with a prescription opioid use disorder received specialty treatment in 2016.
* *Opioid Pills Are Everywhere*: In a ten-year span, drug compa-

nies shipped 20.8 million prescription painkillers to two pharmacies in Williamson, West Virginia, a town with only 2,900 people. It's a similar story in many other communities across the country.

♦ *Opioids Are So Addictive*: About 80% of people who use heroin first misused prescription opioids.

ANSWERS FROM THE LEFT AND RIGHT

THE LEFT: Medicare for All

The ascendant health care idea on the Left is Medicare for All, which would do more than just expand to all Americans the single-payer government program that currently provides health care coverage to 60 million Americans at or over 65. The Medicare for All Act of 2019—which has over 100 House and a dozen Senate cosponsors—would also expand the scope of services covered, limit choice of private insurance and provider options, and eliminate the cost-sharing (premiums, deductibles, co-pays) that helps pay for the current Medicare program.

The left-leaning Urban Institute estimates that Medicare for All would provide coverage to an additional 28 million people but would increase federal health care spending by $3.2 trillion annually over the next 10 years, which is equivalent to about 80% of the entire federal budget in 2018. This topline cost estimate—which has been widely reported in the news—is a bit misleading, however. Because Medicare for All would displace most of the current spending from private insurers and individuals, the same study projects it will increase total health care spending, from all payers, by $660 billion annually over the next ten years.

But these are just estimates, as cost projections for Medicare for All depend upon answers to unknowable questions like:

♦ How will payment rates change for doctors and hospitals?
♦ How much would administrative costs increase or decrease?
♦ How much would utilization of health care services increase?

Program Expansion

However you slice it, Medicare for All would significantly expand a program that is popular and vital for seniors but already on an unsustainable course: Due to our aging population, the Medicare program's enrollment is projected to rise to 79 million by 2030. Medicare's own trustees say the program will no longer be able to pay full benefits by 2026.

Many Medicare beneficiaries find this hard to believe, thinking that they "paid" for their current benefits through payroll taxes. While this is true, they did so only up to a point. The average Medicare beneficiary will receive between $2.40 and $7.80 in Medicare benefits for every $1 they pay in taxes because beneficiaries are living longer and medical treatment is becoming more expensive. In addition, the Medicare payroll taxes Americans pay today are not set aside in a fund for their future care. Instead, the funds are used to pay for the medical care of current retirees.

Elimination of Private Health Insurance

Some Medicare for All advocates also suggest the virtual elimination of private health insurance. But 181 million Americans—or more than half the population—currently get their health care from their employer, and 75% of them believe the health care they receive is "excellent" or "good."

THE RIGHT: Kill Obamacare and Replace It with…TBD

When it comes to health care, the Right knows what it is against: Obamacare. But they haven't yet articulated a workable or coherent vision of what they are for.

In the years after the passage of the Affordable Care Act (Obamacare), House Republicans voted over 70 times to repeal, defund, or modify the law. But when Republicans assumed control of the White House and Congress in 2017, they were never able to pass a replacement for the Affordable Care Act. The plans they did propose—which featured Medicaid block grants and more flexibility for states to opt out of federal regulations—would have significantly increased insurance premiums and reduced coverage, according to independent analysts like the Congressional Budget Office.

The Right has been unable to reckon with a fundamental contradiction. In health care, providing protections and benefits that are popular sometimes requires regulations that are not. For example, 81% of Americans say insurers should be barred from denying coverage to people with preexisting conditions. But if the government forces insurance companies to provide coverage to people who are already sick and require more expensive care, it must also bring more people into the insurance market to prevent price increases for other customers. One way to do this is with an individual mandate that requires everyone to buy health insurance.

These kinds of trade-offs are everywhere in the health care system. But lately, the Right has provided few answers for how to deal with them.

SOLUTIONS:
HEALTH CARE FOR ALL

If there ever was a real debate on whether Washington was responsible for ensuring affordable health care access for all Americans, that debate is essentially over. A February 2019 the Hill-HarrisX poll found that just 15% of Americans want the government to have no role in paying for people's health care. Conversely, just 13% say they'd support Medicare for All if it meant the elimination of private health insurance. The American people are sending a pretty clear message: *We don't want no government and we don't want all government when it comes to health care.* So, what kinds of ideas could bring us closer to real health care for all?

To Expand Access

Address the Doctor Shortage
The Association of American Medical Colleges is predicting a shortage of up to 122,000 physicians by 2030. Closing this gap will entail concerted action at the federal and local levels and in the

private sector. In early 2019, The New Center released a paper with several proposals that could expand the ranks of health care providers in the US.

1. Increase the supply of foreign doctors.

Foreign doctors make up one fourth of the general US physician workforce, and between 2000 and 2013, made up more than 33% of doctors entering the field of family medicine, where shortages are especially acute. But there aren't enough visas available to bring in more foreign practitioners and onerous licensing requirements make it far too difficult for qualified foreign doctors to practice in the US.

2. Streamline medical school curriculums.

A 2012 study published in *JAMA: The Journal of the American Medical Association* found that the length of medical training could be shortened by up to 30% without reducing the quality of the physician.

3. Encourage states to expand the scope of practice of nurse practitioners, physician assistants, and certified nurse midwives.

Nurse practitioners lack full practice rights in 28 US states despite research showing equal levels of both patient satisfaction and health outcomes between patients who saw physicians and patients who saw independent nurse practitioners.

4. Fund the construction of new medical schools and the expansion of old ones.

While federal funding of US medical schools had amounted to 50% of medical schools' revenues in 1965, it made up less than 19% by 2016.

5. Build infrastructure to clear the way for more telemedicine.

In 2014, only 19 states had passed legislation to guarantee telemedicine reimbursement from third-party payers.

To Expand Coverage

IF YOU WANT TO LEAN RIGHT…

Catastrophic Care for All
Instead of Medicare for All, with Washington on the hook for everyone's medical bills, policymakers could consider a version of Catastrophic Care for All. Every American would be enrolled in a high-deductible health care plan that pays for basic preventive care and provides coverage for the catastrophic expenses, like accidents and serious diseases, that drive too many families to bankruptcy. The government could pay for it with a means-tested tax, so those who can't afford the coverage pay nothing.

Let the States Innovate with the Individual Insurance Exchanges
Health policy analyst John C. Goodman believes the fundamental problem in the individual health insurance market is one of risk adjustment in which "health plans in the exchanges are trying to attract the healthy (with low premiums) and avoid the sick (with narrow networks)." He believes this problem could be fixed with changes to federal law that would give states broad authority to allow:

+ Health plans to specialize in the treatment of cancer, diabetes, heart disease, and other conditions and exclude people who do not have these conditions.
+ A market to develop in which plans can bid for the right to treat high-cost health conditions.
+ Medical records to automatically travel with patients from plan to plan.
+ Health plans to ask health questions and conduct medical exams at the time of enrollment.

♦ A market for risk adjustment in which plans compensate other plans when high-cost patients transfer enrollment.

In exchange for being given this flexibility, states would need to:

♦ Have a credible plan to make insurance better for people with chronic health conditions in the form of lower premiums and deductibles and wider networks.
♦ Progress toward a goal where residents who leave the group market and buy their own coverage can find insurance that is comparable in price, quality, and access to care.
♦ Prove its reforms will be revenue neutral for the federal government.

IF YOU WANT TO LEAN LEFT…

Lower the Buy-in Age for Medicare from 65 to 55

Before the Affordable Care Act passed, one in five people aged 55 to 59 and 29% between 60 and 64 were denied coverage for health reasons. Since the passage of the law, Americans can no longer be denied coverage for preexisting conditions but can still struggle to get good coverage in many markets. In addition, Americans can't qualify for Social Security until age 62 or Medicare until 65, which causes the 55-plus population to face challenges affording health care premiums.

Paying to expand Medicare could require an increase in the payroll tax, and administration would be simpler if Americans were automatically enrolled at 55 as Americans aged 65 are today. Although expanding Medicare access to this group would involve costs, it could also benefit younger Americans.

According to a recent article in *Health Affairs*, "Private insurers and employers would no longer be responsible for this [55–64] age group, which would allow private insurers to reduce premiums on younger families because they would have a younger, and typically healthier, pool of people to cover."

The Public Option

The government could create a federally administered public health insurance plan that would be eligible to anyone currently enrolled in Medicaid or an insurance plan through one of the Affordable Care Act exchanges. Some versions of this idea don't call for the creation of a new federally administered insurance plan but instead suggest simply allowing all Americans to buy into Medicare or Medicaid. Private insurance options would continue to exist, and the more than half of Americans who receive coverage through their employer would not see it change.

To Rein in Costs

Medicare is on an unsustainable fiscal course. But proposals to reduce Medicare benefits or transfer it to a premium support model (in which the government gives people a set amount of money to buy private insurance) are deeply unpopular. So the best way to rein in costs for Medicare for the foreseeable future—and for all other private and public payers—is to pursue reforms that can bring the cost of care down throughout the entire health care system.

Other developed countries—like Germany, Japan, and Australia—spend about half as much per person on health care as the US, and often with better outcomes.

Although prescription drugs account for only 10% of all US healthcare expenditures, they are still the most visceral example of high health care costs for many Americans, who pay an average of $1,443 each year for these medicines.

For years, pharmaceutical companies have been saying that high drug prices are necessary to fund new medical innovations. They actually have a point.

Consider that 95% of drug candidates entering clinical trials fail. No other industry faces this challenge. Imagine, for example, if 95% of Apple's consumer device ideas or 95% of Ford's car designs never made it to market. That would destroy their business. But for biopharmaceutical companies, that is the business. Failure is simply inevitable. That's why a 2014 Tufts University study found the average cost to develop a new drug is $2.6 billion. For every successful treatment, researchers have to pay for a lot of failures.

Medical innovation has always been difficult. But now it's getting even harder as researchers face down intractable chronic diseases like multiple sclerosis, rheumatoid arthritis, and various types of cancer. The science is getting tougher and so are the economics as researchers tackle diseases with smaller patient populations where it can be difficult to recoup research investments. And yet, American universities and pharmaceutical companies still manage to churn out breakthrough innovations. In fact, for decades, America has been responsible for more biomedical innovation—new patents and new medicines—than any other country in the world.

So we guess that means the system works and the next president and Congress can't do much about how drugs are priced in the US? Not so fast. Although US pharmaceutical companies do spend billions on R&D, many spend even more on sales and marketing. The pharmaceutical companies' argument that any effort to rein in prices will destroy medical innovation looks a little flimsier when you realize how much money is going to pay for Cialis ads on the nightly news.

As with most issues in the book, both sides of the drug pricing argument really do have merit, and there are no easy answers to the problem of high prices in our medical system. But here are a few solutions to consider, many of which aim to bring more transparency and competition into the health care sector:

Change How Medicaid and Medicare Pay

Despite some recent reforms, Medicare still mostly pays for the volume of care delivered (number of tests and services) rather than the value (improving patient health). Washington should expand experiments with different fee schedules to make Medicare more efficient, like perhaps adding bonuses for physicians who can meet a certain target budget for care.

Medicaid needs the same kinds of reforms. Because states control how Medicaid is run and the federal government pays most of the bills, no one has both the desire and the ability to keep costs in check. States could do it but they don't really care; the federal government may want to do it, but it can't.

Let Medicare Negotiate Prices

The Department of Veterans Affairs does it. Other countries do it. It really makes no sense that Medicare can't negotiate the prices it pays for $129 billion worth of prescription drugs each year. Some people have legitimate concerns about the idea of government bureaucrats in DC arbitrarily setting drug prices. One way to alleviate this concern is to create a fully transparent price index of what other countries pay for medicines, and Medicare would pay some average of it.

Real Price Transparency

In early 2018, the Trump administration's Health and Human Services Department directed all hospitals to post prices for all their services. Hospitals are now doing it, but the information is almost useless. The *New York Times* ran a story in January 2019 listing procedures from various hospital price lists: $42,569 for a cardiology procedure described as "HC PTC CLOS PAT DUCT ART" from Vanderbilt University Medical Center and $9,818 for "Embolza Protect 5.5" from Baptist Health in Miami. In other words, complete gibberish to anyone who isn't a medical professional.

We get it. Health care is complicated and hospital prices and services will never be as simple as a McDonald's menu. But real price transparency—which would allow informed consumers to shop for the best and most affordable care—means lists of prices and services that everyone can understand.

Stop the Crazy Lawsuits

As noted earlier, physicians practicing "defensive medicine"—ordering unnecessary tests and procedures to avoid the possibility of future lawsuits—costs America as much as $100 billion a year, and we all pick up the tab. And according to the Harvard Public School of Health, 40% of medical malpractice suits filed in the US are "without merit." Congress should pursue real tort reform that makes it harder to file frivolous medical lawsuits and potentially cap jury awards.

Curb the Influence of Drug Industry Middlemen

Pharmacy benefit managers (PBMs) play a central role in the current medical ecosystem by representing health insurance plans in negotiations with pharmaceutical companies over drug prices. Theoretically, these PBMs are supposed to negotiate lower prices for their clients (insurers) who can then offer lower premiums or co-pays to Americans who buy health insurance. But many critics say PBMs—which often make exclusive deals with drug makers to favor certain medicines—are limiting the choices for patients and using the discounts they get from drug makers to pad their profits rather than reduce costs for consumers.

In 2019, the Trump administration proposed banning rebates paid by drug makers to PBMs, in government programs like Medicare, with Health and Human Services Secretary Alex Azar accusing PBMs of operating "a hidden system of kickbacks to middlemen" that harms consumers.

The Trump proposal has yet to be finalized as of Spring 2019, and Congress would need to act to ban rebates in the commercial insurance market. At minimum, it is time for real transparency into the practices of PBMs, who claim as trade secrets the complex web of arrangements and contracts they have with drug makers. It's a weak defense and one the president and Congress should take head on.

Don't Let Companies Game the Patent System

Biologic drugs—which are produced from living organisms as opposed to chemical compounds—now account for 40% of all prescription drug spending in the US even though they are only used by 2% of the population. These therapies—like Humira for rheumatoid arthritis and Avastin for cancer—are life changing for many patients but are also prohibitively expensive, with some costing tens or hundreds of thousands of dollars per year.

The companies behind these treatments can get up to 20 years of patent protection before facing competition from "biosimilars," which are the generic versions of biologics. However some biologic manufacturers appear to be gaming the patent system by filing for dozens or even hundreds of new patents—right before their medicine is about to lose its patent exclusivity—covering minor changes that don't represent any real breakthroughs but do have the effect of discouraging biosimilars from coming to market.

A new bipartisan bill—the Biologic Patent Transparency Act— cosponsored by Senators Susan Collins (R-ME) and Tim Kaine (D-VA) would discourage these late-filed patents and require companies to publicly disclose the web of patents that protect their biologics, making it easier for competitors to evaluate and plan for the development of generic versions of these drugs. The bill was moving through Congress but had not yet passed when this book went to print in the summer of 2019.

Answering the End-of-Life Question

Medicare should require every new enrollee to develop an Advance Directive, which is a written statement of a person's wishes regarding medical treatment to ensure those wishes are carried out should the person be unable to communicate them to a doctor. Only 37% of American adults currently have an Advance Directive.

First and foremost, these directives give patients and their families control over how they want to be treated and cared for in their final days. Absent such a directive, many end-of-life patients are subjected to painful and sometimes unwanted care like mechanical ventilation and blood transfusions to keep them alive. But Advance Directives also can play a role in curbing the escalating medical costs for Medicare and for families. One study published in *JAMA* found that the cost of a Medicare patient's final hospitalization was three times higher ($95,505) for patients without Advance Directives compared to those who had one ($30,478).

Critics and cynics often try to demagogue end-of-life discussions by raising the specter of "death panels" killing off the elderly. So let's be clear about what we mean by this proposal. Each person has a right to decide how they want to be treated at the end of their life. If their preference is for any and all measures to be taken to keep them alive, their Advance Directive can make that clear. An Advance Directive is meant above all to give patients and their families control over their care. It just so happens that wider use of Advance Directives will also likely help control health care costs for everyone else.

An Alzheimer's Moon Shot

Dr. Greg Petsko, a professor of neurology and neuroscience with Weill Cornell Medical College, describes Alzheimer's Disease as "the hardest medical problem humankind has ever tried to crack." Despite decades and billions of dollars of research, there are only five treatments available for the disease and all of them only treat symptoms.

The good news is that Congress in 2018 approved the largest ever increase for Alzheimer's and dementia research through the National Institutes of Health. The bad news is that this funding is still short of what researchers require and what other diseases—like cancer and AIDS—receive.

When you consider that Alzheimer's could cost Medicare and Medicaid over $700 billion by midcentury—equivalent to over 15% of the entire federal budget—Washington needs to place a singular priority on finding treatments and a cure for this awful disease.

To Stem the Opioid Epidemic

Treat Addicts Like Patients, Not Criminals

In 2018, Congress passed and President Trump signed several bills that will help reduce prison time for low-level drug offenders and provide resources to combat the opioid epidemic. But considering that opioid abuse may be the biggest public health crisis in the country, the resources we are putting toward it fall woefully short, especially when measured against other government mobilizations to fight scourges like AIDS or cancer. The next president and Congress should make a large investment to provide more beds for rehabilitation and should push for the ability of primary care doctors to prescribe the medication that treats addiction.

To Reduce Medical Errors

Real Data Interoperability

Big electronic health records companies often prevent their competitors from importing patient data by disclosing it in unusable or confusing formats. Washington needs to tear down the walls with legislation that compels these kinds of companies to provide what Cicero Institute Founder Joe Lonsdale describes as an "open application programming interface (API) that will allow an innovation ecosystem of apps, medical devices, and novel insurance plans to flourish."

★2020★
CANDIDATE QUESTIONS

For President Trump

Q1: You said you'd repeal Obamacare and replace it with a better system that provides "insurance for everybody" and that is "far less expensive." You said also there would be no cuts to Medicaid. But most of the plans Republicans proposed in 2018 cut Medicaid spending and reduced coverage. How do you explain this huge disconnect between what you promised on health care and the legislation you actually supported in Congress?

Q2: Republicans controlled the White House, Senate, and the House for two years and never once passed a viable replacement for Obamacare. Why should we trust you will be able to do it in the future?

Q3: Unlike Medicare, the Veterans' Health Administration (VA) negotiates its own drug prices, and as a result they pay 40% less for prescription drugs. Why can't Medicare do the same thing?

Q4: You say you want to protect people with preexisting conditions from insurers who would discriminate against them. But your Justice Department is supporting a state-led lawsuit to declare the protections unconstitutional. How can you say you support these protections when your own Justice Department wants to scrap them?

For Democratic Candidates

Q1: Most people in America get their insurance through their jobs and actually like the care they are getting. Shouldn't we try to improve our current health care system instead of tearing the whole thing down and creating a new one?

Q2: One estimate says Medicare for All would increase national health care spending by $660 billion per year. That's almost 20% of the entire federal budget. How can we afford this?

Q3: Do you believe private health insurance—including the insurance provided by employers—should be eliminated and replaced with a single-payer plan?

Q4: In a 2016 study, researchers found that 28% of Americans smoked, 62% ate an unhealthy diet, and 53% didn't get enough exercise. Before we guarantee unlimited health care for everyone, shouldn't we find ways to make people more responsible for their own health?

Q5: The biggest changes the Affordable Care Act made were to the market for individual insurance. That's where premiums seem to be going up the most. Why is this happening and what will you do to fix it?

For All Candidates

Q1: In the US, medical errors are the third-leading cause of death. How will you fix this problem?

Q2: More people died of drug overdoses in America last year than servicemen during the entire Vietnam War. Congress passed bills last year to combat the opioid crisis, but they did not significantly increase spending on opioid addiction treatment. Will you make fighting drug addiction more of a priority as president, and if so, how?

★5★

ENERGY AND
CLIMATE CHANGE

Climate change used to be a scientific idea. Now it has become a political one; another litmus test for partisans to identify membership in their political tribe. Still, as of late 2018, a Monmouth poll found that eight in ten Americans—including two-thirds of Republicans—believe that climate change is happening and causing extreme weather.

So why is it so impossible for Washington to forge a consensus on how to deal with climate change? Because acknowledging the existence of climate change (as most Americans do) is much easier than agreeing on what to do about it. To understand why, look at this chart of global economic growth over the last 2,000 years that appears on the next page.

For the first 1,800 years, human living standards barely rose at all. And then the Industrial Revolution happened, sparking the greatest increase in human health, well-being, and longevity in history. The Industrial Revolution was spurred on by many things, above all energy, and fossil fuels in particular: first coal and then oil and gas, which were abundant, affordable, and portable. Other energy advances would follow, such as the advent of nuclear power and the harnessing of the hydropower of rivers and streams. Renewable energy use grew exponentially. But today, fossil fuels still account for about 80% of all the world's energy use—which is essentially the same proportion it accounted for 30 years ago.

THE WORLD UNTIL 2000

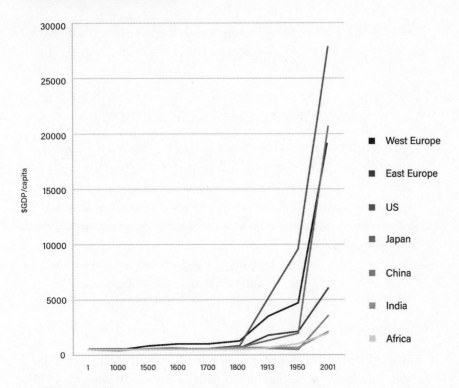

Source: The Atlantic, 2012

So when people talk about fighting climate change, what they are really talking about is redesigning and reengineering the entire economic and energy system that has propelled humanity forward for the last 200 years. It's worth doing. It needs doing. But this chapter will reveal scientific, economic, and political realities that partisans on the extreme Right and Left won't want to hear:

- Climate change is happening, humans are causing it, the risks are growing, and the science behind it is stronger than it has ever been.
- Meeting the goal of eliminating carbon emissions from the US economy by 2030—as called for in the congressional Green New Deal resolution—is simply not achievable given

the scale of the transition and the technological break-throughs still required.

So let's take a look at why the climate change challenge is serious, why there is hope to address it, and why it will still be so hard to solve.

WHY CLIMATE CHANGE IS SERIOUS

"If a baseball player starts taking steroids, he has a much better chance of hitting lots more home runs…Now, that doesn't mean you can point to any particular home run and say aha, that home run is because he's taking steroids, but the pattern…is attributable to his taking steroids. And by analogy I think what we're seeing is weather on…climate steroids."

—Dr. Jane Lubchenco, Former Administrator,
National Oceanic and Atmospheric Administration

1. It's Getting Hotter

Modern global record keeping of weather began in 1880. According to both the National Aeronautics and Space Administration (NASA) and National Oceanic and Atmospheric Administration (NOAA), 17 of the 18 warmest years have occurred since 2001.

2. Natural Disasters Are Getting Worse

In 2017, natural disasters cost the United States $306 billion, a record high. Sixteen of them surpassed a billion dollars in damage each.

3. Seas Are Rising

The equivalent of a football field worth of land disappears from the Louisiana coast every 100 minutes on average.

4. There Is No Real Debate About Whether Climate Change Is Happening

While there is scientific debate about the future costs, risks, and trade-offs of climate change, 97% of published climate research reaches the consensus that climate change is both real and influenced by human activity (although there is not consensus on the precise degree to which human activity or natural causes are responsible). A 2017 study found the other 3% of studies were all in some way flawed in their research and methodology.

5. Human Health Is at Risk

According to the Fourth National Climate Assessment, representing the consensus view of 13 US federal agencies and 300 experts, "Climate change creates new risks and exacerbates existing vulnerabilities in communities across the United States, presenting *growing challenges to human health and safety, quality of life, and the rate of economic growth.*"

6. Increased Resource Competition Could Lead to More Violence

According to a 2014 US Department of Defense Report, "The pressures caused by a climate change will influence resource competition while placing additional burdens on economies, societies, and governance institutions around the world. These effects are threat multipliers that will aggravate stressors abroad such as poverty, environmental degradation, political instability, and social tensions— *conditions that can enable terrorist activity and other forms of violence.*"

WHY THERE IS HOPE

1. Renewables Are Becoming Much More Affordable

Solar and wind costs have dropped 88% and 69% since 2009. In some areas with a lot of sunshine or a lot of wind, the cost of renewables can actually be less than that of fossil fuels.

LOW-END LEVELIZED COST ($/MWH) OF ELECTRICITY BY SOURCE 2018*

ENERGY SOURCE	LOW-END LEVELIZED COST ($/MWH)
Solar (Thin Film Utility Scale)	$36
Wind	$29
Nuclear	$1112
Coal	$60
Natural Gas (Gas Combined Cycle)	$41

2. Renewables Are Providing More of Our Energy

Renewables' share of US energy consumption has doubled since 2008 and now provides 17% of our electricity generation and 11% of our total energy consumption (which includes activities like manufacturing, transportation, etc.). A recent report from the US Department of Energy's Office of Energy Efficiency and Renewable Energy suggests that renewables could supply as much as 80% of total US electricity generation by 2050, using generation technologies currently available today. However, the report also says such an increased share for renewables would require a "more flexible elec-

---

* Low-end Levelized Cost is essentially a measure of what it takes to cost, build, run, and supply different energy facilities nationwide. This measure does not include the cost of transmission and grid integration, which is why costs for various energy sources can differ widely across the country.

ITS ALL ABOUT THE BATTERIES

Batteries make up a third of the cost of an electric vehicle. As battery costs continue to fall, demand for EVs will rise.

Cost for lithium-ion battery packs

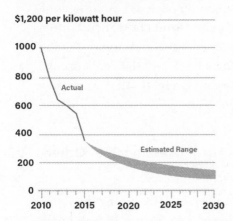

$1,200 per kilowatt hour

Yearly demand for EV battery power

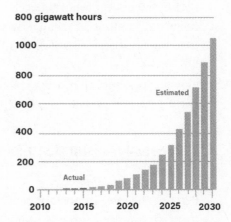

800 gigawatt hours

Data compiled by Bloomberg

tric system," including "flexible conventional generation, grid storage, new transmission, more responsive loads, and changes in power system operations."

3. Energy Storage Is Getting Better

The cost of utility scale energy storage—which is necessary to store power when the sun isn't shining and wind isn't blowing—is falling by 20% per year.

4. US Greenhouse Gas Emissions (GHG) Are Declining

US GHG emissions—which include carbon and other heat-trapping gases like methane—decreased by 2.7% between 2016 and 2017. However, the US is still one of the highest per capita emitters of carbon, as the average American emits about twice as much carbon as the average person in China.

WHY A CLEAN ENERGY FUTURE IS SO HARD TO ACHIEVE

Some think the only thing standing in the way of a perfectly green energy future is oil company lobbyists. And some oil companies did spend years doing what tobacco companies once did: funding junk science to refute real science they thought would hurt their bottom line. But the biggest barrier to a clean energy future today isn't Big Oil. It's the basic laws of physics, economics, and the challenges of global geopolitics that best explain why fossil fuels still rule and why cutting carbon emissions is so challenging.

1. Renewables Still Don't Pack the Power Punch of Other Fuels

Perhaps the most important measurement in determining the viability of an energy source is power density; a measure of how much power you can extract from a unit of volume, energy, or mass. The most relevant metric for renewables is watts per square meter (w/m^2).

How much power can you squeeze out of a given piece of real estate? In the case of renewables, the answer is not much:

ENERGY SOURCE	POWER DENSITY (W/M^2)
Wind	1.2
Solar Photovoltaic	6.7
Oil	28
Nuclear	56

What's the real-world implication of this measurement? Meeting all of America's current electricity needs with wind power would require a land mass twice the size of California.

2. Carbon Dioxide Emitted Today Will Stay in the Atmosphere for Between 20–200 Years

This means that even if the entire world stopped emitting carbon now, climate change will continue because it takes so long to cool off or heat up the oceans and the atmosphere. One study found the Earth's temperature would still increase another 1.1 degrees Celsius even if all emissions from fossil fuels were halted.

3. The Wind Isn't Always Blowing, and the Sun Isn't Always Shining

Every electric utility in America has one mandate above all: always keep the lights on. To do it, they need something called "baseload" power, which means power that will always be there when they need it, like for hot days when energy usage spikes because everyone is blasting their air conditioner. The best measurement for an energy source's ability to meet this standard is capacity factor, which measures how long an energy source can deliver maximum power over a given period.

So, here's what the below chart means: Let's imagine an electric utility has a 1,000-megawatt nuclear reactor. Because nuclear has a capacity factor that is about three and a half times that of solar, that utility would need to build 3,500 megawatts (3.5 × 1,000) worth of

CAPACITY FACTORS FOR UTILITY SCALE GENERATORS 2016

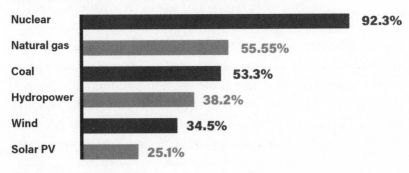

Nuclear — 92.3%
Natural gas — 55.55%
Coal — 53.3%
Hydropower — 38.2%
Wind — 34.5%
Solar PV — 25.1%

Source: U.S. Energy Information Administration

solar capacity to reliably deliver the same amount of power to its customers as the 1,000-megawatt nuclear reactor. And that may understate it, because remember: the sun isn't always shining.

4. Steel Can't Be Made Without Fossil Fuels

Steelmaking accounts for 7% of all global carbon emissions. Although there are a few pilot projects exploring new ways to make steel—one in Sweden is using hydrogen harnessed from renewables—71% of the world's steel is made with coal, with natural gas accounting for most of the rest. Heavy industry—like steelmaking—accounts for a quarter of all US greenhouse gas emissions and is even more dependent on fossil fuels than other sectors, like transportation and electricity generation.

5. Nuclear Power Is on the Decline

Nuclear power provides 20% of America's electrical output and is our largest source of carbon-free energy. But nuclear power's high upfront costs and declining political support—it is not included at all in the Green New Deal proposal for example—is jeopardizing its future in the US. A recent study found that "nearly 35% of the country's nuclear power plants...are at risk of early closure or slated for retirement to retire." The report goes on to say that if this happens "natural gas and coal will fill the void."

6. The Geopolitics

The US accounts for only 15% of global carbon emissions, and even as the US decreases its own emissions, other countries—particularly China—are increasing theirs. Put aside the coal-fired power plants China already has. The hundreds of new coal plants China is building now will equal the output of all coal plants in the US. Solar and wind power still account for only about 2% of all global energy use.

2014 GLOBAL CO$_2$ EMISSIONS FROM FOSSIL FUEL COMBUSTION AND SOME INDUSTRIAL PROCESSES

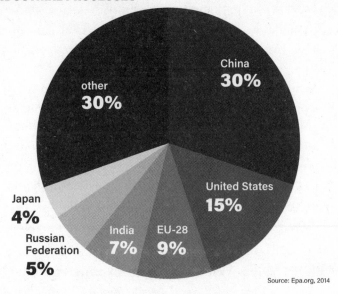

Source: Epa.org, 2014

7. One in Six of the World's People Still Do Not Have Access to Electricity

That's some 1.2 billion people who live in a state of "energy poverty," without access to lights, appliances, and countless necessities the rest of the world takes for granted. Many people without access to electricity rely on polluting or dangerous energy sources like kerosene or burning wood in their homes. Many developing countries around the world still see low-cost fossil fuels as the most economical way to bring their people out of energy poverty.

ANSWERS FROM THE LEFT AND RIGHT

THE LEFT: Green New Deal

As noted in the opening of this book, the Green New Deal is more than just a plan to fight climate change. It is a comprehensive framework that envisions Washington exerting control over large sectors of the economy and society to fight climate change and economic and social injustice. Even the goals specific to climate and energy are staggering in their ambition and impracticality. The text of the House resolution calling for the creation of a Select Committee for the Green New Deal envisions Washington directing an effort to:

+ Achieve "net zero" carbon emissions within ten years;
+ Upgrade "every residential and industrial building for state-of-the-art energy efficiency, comfort, and safety." (There are about 100 million residential and 6 million commercial buildings in the US.);
+ Decarbonize "the manufacturing, agricultural, and other industries" along with "transportation and other infrastructure."

THE RIGHT: "Global Warming Is an Expensive Hoax!"
(Tweet from Donald Trump, January 2014)

President Trump has since walked back this statement a bit, conceding climate change may be happening. But climate change skepticism still runs deep on the Right. As recently as 2008, Republican presidential candidate John McCain not only admitted the threat of climate change but put forth a policy platform for a national cap and trade system to reduce carbon emissions. Today, too many on the Right believe climate change doesn't exist, that the risks are overstated, or that if it is indeed a problem, it is someone else's problem.

SOLUTIONS:
ENERGY INNOVATION

The Right wants to ignore climate change. The Left wants to radically disrupt virtually every part of America's economy and society to fight it. Neither approach makes sense.

Climate change is exacting a real cost on our economy and environment now, and if the Right doesn't end its relentless—and indefensible—climate denial, the costs will keep adding up. But the

Left's utopian vision to fight climate change could create large costs too. Consider that if household energy costs went up just 10%, it would push almost 840,000 Americans into poverty.

What if the Green New Deal turns out to be much more expensive and disruptive than its advocates suggest? There are more than a few government initiatives that fit that description.

Battling climate change is a multidecade challenge, which means it needs to be sustained across multiple presidencies and Congresses. If recent history is any guide, that will include periods with unified Republican and Democratic control as well as divided government. That's why any climate change solution—to have any chance to last—must be forged in the center with buy-in from both parties.

So what to do? Ironically, the solution to a cleaner energy future may be found in our fossil fuel past.

In the early 2000s, energy experts were sounding a dire warning. The US was running out of oil and gas. A popular book released at the time was called *The End of Oil*, and it reflected the growing conventional wisdom that global supplies of crude oil would soon peak, bringing an era of soaring energy prices and economic upheaval. In 2003, the *Oil and Gas Journal* reported the United States had just 22.5 billion barrels of proven oil reserves. But today the US is estimated to have 264 billion barrels of proven oil reserves—more than Saudi Arabia or Russia.

So how did America actually increase our oil reserves by a factor of more than ten, even as we were consuming billions of barrels of oil in the last 15 years?

Technology. An advanced drilling technique called *fracking* allowed us to access energy we never thought we could reach.

When government lays the foundation for innovation and the private sector is empowered to build on that foundation, new products come to market, new jobs are created, and new solutions are found to old problems. This approach is how a president governing from the center could attack the climate change challenge. China and India are not building hundreds of new coal plants because they intend to destroy the world. They are doing it because it's often the cheapest way to power their economies and to pull people out of poverty. This will not change until energy alternatives or technologies emerge that provide the same thing that coal and other fossil fuels do for these countries: cheap, abundant, and affordable power on a massive scale.

☆ THE FRACKING REVOLUTION ☆

In July 2013, George P. Mitchell—the founder of Mitchell Energy—passed away at the age of 94. In his obituary, the Associated Press called Mitchell the "Father of Fracking" and credited him with sparking the American shale gas revolution. In the AP story, Mitchell's family described a "quintessentially American" story of someone who rose from nothing to become a great entrepreneur and energy innovator. Mitchell was indeed a trailblazer, and he deserved all the accolades he received. But he had some help. From the federal government.

Although Mitchell's company came to market in the 1990s with a revolutionary fracking technique, it also drew on technology that was invented, funded, or subsidized by Uncle Sam. To cite just two examples: Sandia National Laboratories developed the seismic modeling and imaging technology that allowed Mitchell to more precisely locate oil and gas reserves. Meanwhile, the US Department of Energy funded joint ventures that ultimately produced the diamond-tipped drilling bits and pioneered horizontal drilling techniques that were later adapted for commercial use by Mitchell Energy. In fact, Dan Steward, a former Mitchell Energy VP, told the nonpartisan Breakthrough Institute that the "DOE [Department of Energy] started it, and other people took the ball and ran with it. You cannot diminish DOE's involvement."

The lesson here is that government can play a critical role in funding the basic energy research that is too long-range, risky, or expensive for the private sector to handle alone. It's true in other industries as well, as breakthrough technologies ranging from GPS and the internet to memory foam mattresses got their start in government research labs.

It may take an inventor or a company creating solar or wind technologies that are exponentially more efficient at converting sun and wind into power. Or a battery that can efficiently and affordably store huge amounts of energy. Or smaller, safer, more affordable nuclear reactors. Or a scalable technology that can pull carbon straight out of the air.

How about we create those technologies in the US? The goal of our next president's energy policy should be to evolve America's energy system to rely more on cleaner, cost-effective sources that are sustainable without unnecessarily disrupting our economy and our way of life.

Two big policy ideas stand out for the next president.

1. Double Down on Federal R&D into Breakthrough Energy Technologies

According to the Pew Charitable Trust, energy investments have accounted for only 1% of the federal government's R&D budget since the 1990s. By comparison, defense has received almost half of federal research money, and health has consumed 20%–25%.

Although the federal government does have an entity—ARPA-E, or the Advanced Research Projects Agency-Energy—to fund investments in breakthrough energy technologies, it needs significantly more funding to explore and invest in potential breakthrough energy technologies. These could include:

+ Technologies that capture carbon produced at fossil fuel plants and store it underground (carbon capture and storage), and technologies that pull existing carbon out of the air
+ Advanced energy and battery storage
+ Next generation and modular (smaller) nuclear reactors
+ Climate mitigation and adaptation technologies (e.g., geo-engineering, building and electric grid resiliency, etc.) that can help blunt the impacts of climate change that are already happening

2. Put a Price on Carbon...and Put the Money in People's Pockets

Carbon tax. Gas tax. Whatever you call it, voters tend to hate it. Any policy that increases the cost for people to fuel up their cars is seen as a political nonstarter. In late 2018, people rioted in the streets of Paris after French President Emmanuel Macron announced a new fuel tax. But the basic idea behind a carbon tax is sound. If companies have to pay for emitting carbon, they are more likely to invest in new technologies that reduce carbon emissions or emit none at all. It's government's way of encouraging more clean energy investment without being too prescriptive about telling innovators how to do it.

One way to have a carbon tax without the politically toxic blowback could be to place a steadily rising fee on fossil fuels but rebate the dividends from this fee directly back to US households each month (sometimes called "carbon fee and dividend") or as part of their annual tax returns. Seeing that carbon dividend could go a long way toward assuring voters they aren't on the losing end of any carbon tax policy. With a carbon fee in place, many of the complicated and burdensome environmental rules and regulations in place to reduce emissions could potentially be loosened or eliminated.

There are many ways to design such a program, and the politics will always be hard. But the energy innovation America and the world needs will be much more achievable if the market sends a signal that cleaner investments will be more appealing and carbon intensive investments will be less appealing over time.

★2020★
CANDIDATE QUESTIONS

For President Trump

Q1: The US Defense Department says climate change puts two-thirds of US military installations at risk. And 13 different federal agencies just released a report stating that climate change is real and already harming our country. Why don't you agree with them?

Q2: Coal is declining as a share of US energy, and many people say the biggest reason is because natural gas is just a cheaper and cleaner fuel. So why is a Republican president—who is supposed to support free markets—doing so much to prop up the failing coal industry?

For Democratic Candidates

Q1: Do you support the Green New Deal? And if you do, what exactly do you mean by that? Does it mean you support the resolution introduced in Congress by Rep. Alexandria Ocasio-Cortez (D-NY)? Or does it mean something else?

Q2: Renewable energy provides about 11% of all the power in the US. The Green New Deal calls for increasing this by a factor of almost ten over ten years. Can you explain how this is remotely possible?

For All Candidates

Q1: Would you consider supporting a carbon fee and dividend policy, which would place a rising fee on fossil fuels but rebate the dividends from this fee directly back to US households?

★ 6 ★

INFRASTRUCTURE

n late 2018, Ryan was driving on the Brooklyn-Queens Expressway and suddenly felt a jolt. Car, meet pothole. A $1,800 mechanic's bill later and he had received a stark reminder that America's infrastructure is pretty terrible. And yet, Ryan got off easy. He didn't get hurt. He could pay the bill. It was an inconvenience, not a crisis.

Many Americans and many communities are not that lucky. In 2014, Americans reacted with horror when we learned that Flint, Michigan—due to chronic underinvestment and mismanagement—had exposed its residents to unconscionably high levels of lead in their water. Children in Flint suffered brain and development damage from which they will never recover.

It's outrageous. Every year the American Society of Civil Engineers (ASCE) provides a report card with letter grades on the quality of various American infrastructure.

- ◆ Aviation: D
- ◆ Drinking Water: D
- ◆ Roads: D
- ◆ Transit: D-

Our rail system got a B, the highest score of any infrastructure. But the overall grade? D+.

We can and must do a lot better. America's decaying infrastructure is costing jobs, it is costing lives, and it is long past due for an overhaul.

THE PROBLEM:
AMERICA'S INFRASTRUCTURE
IS BROKEN AND OUTDATED

Here are five reasons why we should all pay attention:

1. We Are Losing Time and Money

Bad roads cost Americans $500 every year in car repairs and wasted fuel.

- In 2014, the average American spent 42 hours delayed in traffic.

2. Our Resources Are Being Wasted

Leaks and breaks cost water systems between 6% and 25% of their water, wasting over 7 billion gallons of water each day, or enough to fill about 11,000 Olympic swimming pools.

3. Our Health Is Being Jeopardized

Almost 900 million gallons of untreated sewage, which can include human feces and wastewater from daily activities, are discharged each year due to aging pipes and inadequate capacity. This is enough sewage to fill over 11 million bathtubs.

- In Flint, water testing in 2014 showed lead levels that were as much as hundreds of times higher than the Environmental Protection Agency's allowable limit.
- Flint is not an isolated example. Of states that reported lead testing results in 2014, 40% had higher rates of lead poisoning among children than Flint.

4. Communities Are Being Left Behind in the Race for 21st-Century Jobs

Thirty-eight percent of rural Americans don't have access to high-speed internet, and about 6.5 million students in rural K–12 schools don't have access to it either.

* Why does this matter? Because studies show that people who live in states with high-speed internet make more money and have higher college graduation rates than those who don't.

5. Jobs Are Being Destroyed

Global consulting firm McKinsey estimates that increasing US infrastructure spending by 1% of the GDP would add 1.5 million jobs to the economy. Not investing in infrastructure will do the opposite; by 2025, deteriorating infrastructure will cost some 2.5 million jobs.

WHY IS IT SO BAD?

1. Decades of Underinvestment

The ASCE estimates the US is spending about $200 billion per year less than it should to get our infrastructure up to a B grade.

* As a share of the economy, Europe spends twice as much and China spends five times as much as the US on infrastructure.

2. A Tangle of Red Tape

According to Common Good, a nonprofit that has spent years advocating for fixes to the process for building infrastructure, "Permitting for infrastructure projects can take a decade or more. Multiple agencies oversee the process, with no clear lines of authority. Once permits are granted, lawsuits can last years more. These delays are costly and, often, environmentally destructive."

☆ WHERE DOES INFRASTRUCTURE ☆ FUNDING COME FROM?

Of the $416 billion in public money spent in 2014 on infrastructure, about a quarter came from the federal government and three-fourths from states and localities. According to the Congressional Budget Office (CBO), "of the federal spending, roughly two-thirds paid for new, improved, or rehabilitated structures and equipment. State and local governments spent money on those things as well, but a much larger proportion of their spending paid for the operation and maintenance of infrastructure."

Amid the deficit in public infrastructure spending, private investment is filling some of the void. In 2018, investors funneled a record of $85 billion in private equity and debt funds focused on US and global infrastructure.

ANSWERS FROM THE LEFT AND RIGHT

Here is the good news: Most on the Left and Right agree that America's decrepit infrastructure is a real problem that needs fixing.

The bad news: They can't agree how to pay for it. In 2018, Republicans and Democrats in Washington released competing infrastructure plans that read more as political documents than serious policy proposals.

THE LEFT: A Lot of New Public Investment

In 2018, Senate Democrats proposed a $1 trillion federal investment in infrastructure, which would have been paid for by repealing many of the tax cuts President Trump had signed into law months earlier. No matter what you think of the 2017 tax cut package, expecting President Trump to agree to a plan that eliminates his signature domestic achievement is just as unrealistic as when congressional Republicans proposed budget deals that would have required President Obama to defund his own signature domestic achievement, the Affordable Care Act.

It's not going to happen.

THE RIGHT: A Little Public Investment to Spur Private Investment

In 2018, the Trump administration unveiled a $200 billion infrastructure investment plan, which they claimed would spur $1.5 trillion in new private sector infrastructure investments. But the plan had a fatal flaw. Private investors are only interested in infrastructure projects that can generate an economic return. Many of the most critical infrastructure priorities in America—like fixing old water pipes and filling potholes—fall into the category of "deferred maintenance," which almost always require public investment.

According to the Congressional Budget Office, "almost all spending on transportation, drinking water, and wastewater infrastructure is done by the public sector."

SOLUTIONS:
REAL FUNDING AND REAL FLEXIBILITY

Not only is America not building the infrastructure we will need for the next half-century, we are not even maintaining what we have built in the past half-century. Our infrastructure needs are immense and undoubtedly require more investment than public financing alone can provide. Any significant infrastructure package will require public and private financing. But it will also require cutting through an incomprehensible morass of red tape, in which new infrastructure projects can sometimes require approval from literally dozens of federal, state, and local agencies. Projects that take two years to build in Europe can take a decade or more in the US.

How to Fund It

- *User Fees*—such as a freight tax—should play an increased role in paying for public infrastructure. It is only fair that people who rely on this infrastructure—and most of us do—will help pay to maintain and improve it.
- *Public-Private Partnerships*: Publicly owned infrastructure that creates residual cash flows comparable to private entities—such as airports, ports, toll roads, and utilities—should be considered for transfer to private ownership, with sale proceeds used to reduce government deficits and liabilities or to reinvest in public infrastructure that does not appeal to private investors.
- *Interstate Highway Tolls*: In 1956, Congress banned the use of tolls on interstate highways. A proposal from the Reason Foundation would reverse this ban provided that states embrace a series of customer-friendly reforms including applying the tolls to all cars and trucks regardless of origin and agreeing to only use the funds for interstate highway repair and operation.
- *Corporate Income Tax*: A one percentage point increase in the corporate income tax—which dropped from 35% to 21% in the 2017 tax reform—would generate $100 billion over 10 years that could be funneled to infrastructure investment.
- *Institutional Investment*: Innovative financing mechanisms—such as Build America Bonds, Private Activity Bonds, and more institutional (e.g., pension fund) investments—should play an expanded role in financing new projects.
- *Individual Equity*: Infrastructure investment should be opened to individuals, not just institutions, by creating more equity instruments that allow individual investors to participate in infrastructure investment via mutual funds, ETFs, and/or 401(k)s.

Cutting Through the Red Tape Jungle

* *Incentivize States to Streamline*: A study by Common Good found that red-tape delays for infrastructure more than double the cost of large projects. Because state and local regulatory hurdles are often the primary barrier to building new infrastructure, federal infrastructure funding should be contingent upon states and localities streamlining their permitting and regulatory processes.
* *More Flexibility at the State Level*: Too much federal infrastructure funding is allocated with overly prescriptive rules as to where states should spend the money. States should be given more flexibility to spend federal infrastructure funding on the projects that they deem to be most important.

Priorities, Priorities

In a time of constrained resources, the federal government must develop better processes to focus investment on the infrastructure projects that are most essential to public safety and economic competitiveness. Too much infrastructure spending occurs because a politician wants their name on a building. Other spending—like California's recently canceled $77 billion high-speed rail project—is done without the proper diligence to determine what communities actually need.

A Capital Budget

Many states and localities, and almost all businesses, have two separate budgets: operational and capital. Roughly speaking, the operational budget pays recurring expenses like utility bills and salaries. The capital budget pays for investments in the future. It's a small but critically important distinction.

Infrastructure is a capital investment because it helps create jobs and stimulate economic activity. So if the US Congress spends $1 on a new road, the Treasury can get some of that back from future tax returns from new economic activity.

But the US Congress doesn't have a capital budget, which means every dollar it spends is treated the same for accounting purposes. This has the effect of decreasing the amount of infrastructure spending. The details can be tough to work out, but Congress should find a way to implement a capital budget that considers return on investment (cost vs. benefit) as a means for making funding decisions.

★2020★
CANDIDATE QUESTIONS

For President Trump

Q1: In your 2018 State of the Union, you promised to "build gleaming new roads, bridges, highways, railways, and waterways across our land." It hasn't happened. Why not?

Q2: Your infrastructure plan calls for the private sector to do much of the investment, but private investors typically don't want to spend money on the boring but essential projects like repairing old roads and water pipes. Why are you so reluctant to put real public money into infrastructure?

For Democratic Candidates

Q1: It costs more in the US to build new infrastructure projects than anywhere else in the world, and much of this is due to corrupt or inefficient bureaucracies that have onerous environmental regulations. Even President Obama said that when it comes to public works, "there is no such thing as shovel-ready projects." What is your plan to fix this problem?

For All Candidates

Q1: America has two big infrastructure needs. We need to fix and repair much of what we already have. But we also need to invest in new infrastructure that will let us compete in the 21st century. Which kind of infrastructure investment should be our highest priority?

Q2: Far too many communities—in rural and economically disadvantaged urban areas—don't have access to high-speed internet and other technologies they need to launch businesses and get good jobs. What is your plan to address this disparity?

Q3: What is your plan to pay for significant new infrastructure investment?

_____

_____

_____

_____

_____

_____

_____

_____

_____

_____

_____

_____

_____

_____

_____

_____

_____

_____

_____

_____

_____

_____

_____

_____

_____

_____

_____

_____

_____

_____

_____

_____

★ 7 ★

THE RISE
OF BIG TECH

n 2010, then-Google CEO Eric Schmidt made an offhand joke
that now seems deadly serious. Appearing at a conference at the
Newseum in Washington, DC, he was asked a question about
whether Google planned to eventually implant technology in people's brains. He said they did not and, in explaining why, said:
"There is what I call the creepy line. The Google policy on a lot of
things is to get right up to the creepy line and not cross it."

Is there any doubt that Google and some other big tech companies have now crossed this line? In recent years, large technology
companies have been investigated for colluding with a secret agreement not to hire one another's best workers; fined billions of dollars
for unfairly favoring certain services on their platforms over other
rivals; and accused of mishandling sensitive consumer information
or obtaining new customers under false pretenses.

Most troubling of all, Americans' private lives suddenly don't
seem so private, as companies—in the tech sector and elsewhere—
have more information than ever before on what we're doing, where
we're doing it, and with whom. In a June 2018 Pew Research Center
poll, 75% of respondents said major tech firms weren't doing enough
to protect the personal data of their users. Consumers love the ease
with which Google allows us to search, Amazon to buy, and Facebook to connect. But the growing dominance of these tech compa-

nies and the platforms they control is coming at a real cost to our privacy and potentially to workers and the economy.

Not long ago, companies like Amazon, Google, and Facebook were scrappy upstarts, creating new industries and disrupting old ways. Today, emerging research suggests these companies could be preventing other new businesses from doing the same thing. In previous eras, a robust legislative or regulatory response to concentrated corporate power was often spurred by widespread public anger. But for a long time, the Big Five technology companies (Apple, Alphabet [parent company of Google], Amazon, Facebook, Microsoft) were viewed favorably by many consumers, with each making regular appearances in the top ten of Fortune's annual list of the World's Most Admired Companies.

And why shouldn't they be? Each has pioneered world-changing innovations and created great fortunes and great jobs. If you are one of the millions who own an S&P 500 index fund in your 401(k), you can thank the Big Five technology companies for as much as a third of the fund's recent gains. These companies have competed and acted in their own interests, which is exactly what we expect in a free-market system. But as these companies have grown, some have also been more prone to engaging in the grungier anticompetitive or acquisitive practices that the public and political leaders decry when practiced in other industries.

The power of technology companies presents government with a challenge very different from the corporate monopolies of the past. These companies don't just dominate a commodity, as Standard Oil did before it was broken up by the Supreme Court in 1911, or physical infrastructure as AT&T did with telephone lines before it was split into the "Baby Bells" in 1984. They own an unprecedented amount of data, the most valuable asset in the world today. And the more data they own, the more powerful they become.

Owning lots of data isn't the problem. What some of these companies are doing with the data—like selling it and sharing it with third parties without their customer's permission—most certainly is.

There is no easy answer to the challenges posed by tech companies, in part because these companies have very different business models. Apple and Microsoft, for example, generate most of their revenues from the sale of hardware, software, and services, while Google and Facebook rely on mostly free services to fuel revenue from ad sales.

It isn't yet clear how to rectify the challenges posed by the rise of large technology companies. But it is abundantly clear that the status quo just won't do.

PROBLEM #1:
THEY KNOW EVERYTHING ABOUT US

- Facebook, Apple, and Google can track your location constantly, even when you are not using an app that explicitly requires location.
- Google keeps track of your location even after you turn off location services in your Google account.
- 70% of the apps on your smartphone share personal data with third-party tracking companies. Phone carriers like T-Mobile, Sprint, and AT&T are also selling location data even after they promised they wouldn't—and it's ending up in the hands of shady third parties like bail bondsmen and bounty hunters.
- Facebook circumvented Federal Trade Commission rules and gave Spotify and Netflix "read and write" access to users' private Facebook messages without explicit consent.

PROBLEM #2:
THEY INTENTIONALLY MAKE IT HARDER FOR CUSTOMERS TO PROTECT THEIR OWN PRIVACY

In its 2018 report, The New Center explored the lengths that consumers must go to safeguard their personal information. According to the report:

> For many websites, privacy is not the default. To protect information online, consumers must dig through confusing privacy settings. Al-

though sites like Facebook now feature pop-ups encouraging us to review our privacy settings, the choices can be overwhelming, and it is often easier and faster to skip through them.

Tech companies actively try to discourage us from protecting our personal information. Instead of allowing us to disable all data collection with one click, we must disable each type of data collection individually. Sometimes it takes more than one change to keep a single type of data private, and the options are not always intuitive. For example, Google allows us to keep our location data private, but its privacy settings are misleading. Disabling the "location history" setting is not enough; another hidden setting, "web and app activity," must also be disabled to prevent Google from tracking location.

To make your Google account completely private, you must disable the following settings:

1. Web & App Activity
2. Location History
3. Device Information
4. Voice & Audio Activity
5. YouTube Search History
6. YouTube Watch History
7. Ad Personalization

As for Facebook…If you choose to allow every type of data collection, it takes five clicks to return to the news feed and continue using Facebook. If you choose to manage your data settings and deny access at each step, it takes eight additional clicks to return to Facebook.

PROBLEM #3:
THEY DOMINATE THEIR MARKETS LIKE FEW COMPANIES IN HISTORY

- 94% of social media users have an account with Facebook or a company owned by Facebook.
- 92% of internet search is controlled by Google.

- 99% of mobile operating systems in the US are made by Apple or Google. By comparison, Standard Oil had 87% of the crude oil market share at its peak.
- One out of every two dollars spent online goes through Amazon.
- Eight of the ten most popular smartphone apps are made by Facebook or Google.

HOW DID THIS HAPPEN?

Only two of the five largest technology companies even existed 25 years ago. Unsurprisingly, regulators and legislators have usually played catch-up in their attempts to govern these businesses, which pioneered industries that never existed before.

In the early years of the internet, Congress and successive presidents made a sensible decision to be relatively hands off in regulating tech companies for fear that too much of it could inhibit the growth and innovation of new companies.

It was probably the right call at the time. But these tech companies are all grown up and simply need to meet a higher standard of public accountability. Aside from long-standing privacy concerns, Left, Right, and Center are also increasingly worried about the immense role that social media companies have in shaping (and sometimes arbitrarily censoring) the news and information we read.

Technology companies are being much more proactive in dealing with concerns about consumer privacy and their business practices, but so much more needs to be done.

ANSWERS FROM THE LEFT AND RIGHT

For a long time, big technology companies escaped more serious scrutiny because neither the Left nor Right were particularly interested in policing them, even though they had different reasons.

THE LEFT: Big Tech Is the Golden Exception

Historically the Left has loved to hate certain kinds of big businesses, like those in oil, pharmaceuticals, and banking. But even as tech companies became even more influential than companies in these other sectors, the Left gave them a pass, believing tech companies were different; an example of a different kind of business that was "doing well while doing good."

THE RIGHT: Let the Market Decide

Historically the Right has been generally averse to regulating businesses of any kind.

But now advocates on the Left, Right, and Center are finding common cause and calling for more aggressive measures to protect consumer privacy online and to address the growing monopoly position of tech companies in certain markets.

There are some issues—like health care and climate change—where the Right and Left are miles apart, not just from one another but from the political center. The growing influence of technology companies is not one of these issues. There is a gathering consensus we need to do something, even if the shape of it isn't clear yet.

SOLUTIONS:
TAKE ON BIG TECH

In Washington, we have the Federal Drug Administration to ensure the safety of new drugs; the Federal Reserve to ensure the soundness of the financial system; and the Securities and Exchange Commission to protect the integrity of markets. Who is in charge of protecting our privacy and policing the actions of big tech companies?

No one, really. Though the Federal Trade Commission (FTC) has some oversight responsibility, they often lack rule-making authority and the necessary money and manpower.

The challenge posed by the rise of big tech companies is among the most consequential facing the next president. We need laws and a regulatory structure that are up to that challenge. The next president will have to tread carefully, as there are many ways that Washington could make things worse. For starters, the technology sector is constantly changing and solutions that Congress might develop in regulations today might be completely ill-equipped to deal with the problems the public will face tomorrow, such as the rise of artificial intelligence.

Washington must also be mindful that even as American tech companies have engaged in troubling behavior, they are still crown jewels of American innovation, fueling economic growth, investment, and job creation. Ill-advised or ineffective regulation might do little to preserve our privacy or improve competition while hurting US tech companies and providing an opening for foreign companies—like those in China—to outcompete us.

But the status quo just isn't acceptable. And if the next president is interested in reckoning with the implication of the rise of big tech, he or she might consider the following:

Congress Needs to Get Smart on Tech

Recent congressional hearings featuring tech company executives have revealed that too many members of Congress don't understand how big tech companies operate or the scope and scale of the problems they present. In one infamous example from 2018, a senator grilling Facebook CEO Mark Zuckerberg at a hearing did not appear to know that the company made money by selling advertisements.

Bring Back the OTA
Once, Congress had a resource for objective analysis on pressing matters raised by new technologies, the Office of Technology Assessment. The OTA was shuttered in 1995, right before the advent of the modern internet. It needs to be brought back to ensure our leaders understand how technology is changing and what it means for America, and the next president should include it in their first budget request to Congress.

To Protect People's Privacy

Federal Privacy Legislation

Large tech companies have every incentive to collect as much personal data as possible from their consumers. Comprehensive federal privacy legislation should be enacted to give consumers more control over their personal data, and it should include: a "right to be removed" from the database of an online platform; opt-out mechanisms for data sales and third-party data use; data collection disclosure; a right to request all personal data collected by companies; and prompt data breach notifications. Although tech companies have understandably been in the spotlight for their privacy practices, strong privacy protections are just as essential for consumer data held by companies in the health care, retail, and other sectors.

Right now, every state has a data breach notification law on the books that provides consumers with a modicum of notice after their internet privacy has been violated, but tech companies have been successful at the state level in preventing the passage of stronger data privacy laws. Additionally, many of the state laws that have been passed are inconsistent with one another. For example, many states have begun enacting legislation related to online security breaches, but some are preventative while others are reactive.

Some tech companies—Apple in particular—have recently come out in favor of federal privacy standards similar to those that now exist in Europe. Is this born out of sincere concern for consumer privacy? Or a pragmatic preference for one national privacy law instead of various competing state versions?

It's hard to say. But any federal privacy law must be carefully crafted to ensure it doesn't put an undue burden on smaller firms. The Facebooks of the world can afford to hire scores of compliance professionals to help them comply with regulations. Many smaller companies can't.

Ethical Standards for Artificial Intelligence

Here's a thought experiment: A self-driving car is moving down the highway when a deer suddenly appears in the road. If the car veers right, it will hit a barrier and likely kill the driver. If it veers left, it will likely save the driver but kill a pedestrian on the sidewalk.

Which decision does the car make? And how does it make it? These are the kinds of thorny ethical questions our society will increasingly be confronted with as artificial intelligence is able to assume more roles and responsibilities in the years ahead.

AI Federal Commission

The next president should create a National Commission on Artificial Intelligence to help provide recommendations for how to navigate the ethical questions around AI. It can be modeled on the President's Council on Bioethics (created by President Bill Clinton) and the National Bioethics Advisory Commission (created by President George W. Bush), which studied and advised on the implications of medical advances like cloning and stem cell research.

Real Transparency

Large tech companies claim they are being more transparent about how they handle your data and decide which content can exist on their platforms, but often they just provide the illusion of compliance, with long, impenetrable terms of service or standards that no one reads.

At a minimum the next president and Congress should make clear that they expect large tech companies to agree upon and adhere to common standards that establish a clear, standardized process for reviewing and removing material from online platforms.

To Promote Competition

Approach "Safe Harbor" with Caution

In 1996, Congress passed a "Safe Harbor" provision to protect early internet companies from litigation—so a company like AOL could not be held liable if someone posted offensive material on one of its chat boards. It was a critical safeguard allowing the nascent internet economy to grow. Now, Congress is taking an interest in whether big technology companies are using Safe Harbor to evade accountability for what goes on their platforms. However, lawmakers must be careful; clumsy changes to Safe Harbor laws to target big tech could instead unfairly impact smaller platforms without the resources to handle increased legal exposure for the content on their sites.

Better Laws

The major US laws governing competition—such as the Sherman Act of 1890—were passed over a century ago. Items for possible inclusion in new legislation could include:

- Addressing the ways that digital companies are using network effects to crowd out potential competitors.
- Redefining and cracking down on predatory pricing practices.
- Tougher scrutiny of mergers that threaten competition within sectors.
- Enacting new rules and procedures to speed up antitrust litigation, which sometimes drags on for a decade or more.

Better Enforcement of Existing Laws

In 1997, the US Justice Department sued Microsoft, claiming it was illegally leveraging its dominant operating system to "develop a chokehold" on the internet browser software market. The government has brought no case of similar size and impact in the last 20 years.

The decline in antitrust enforcement can be traced back to a legal theory first popularized by Robert Bork—a University of Chicago professor and later Supreme Court nominee—that the government should only be concerned with inhibiting a company's size if it is harming "consumer welfare." In practice, this has meant government being hands off so long as prices are low.

Since many big technology companies have, to date, delivered lower-cost or even free services, they have escaped scrutiny of their other practices—like violating consumer privacy and inhibiting competition—that the government should have an interest in addressing.

★2020★
CANDIDATE QUESTIONS

For President Trump

Q1: You tweeted that "Facebook, Twitter, and Google are so biased towards the Dems it is ridiculous!" What is your evidence for that, and what do you want to do about it?

_____

_____

_____

_____

_____

_____

_____

_____

_____

_____

_____

_____

_____

_____

_____

_____

_____

For Democratic Candidates

Q1: The tech industry—and its employees—have donated much more to Democratic candidates than Republican ones. Can we trust Democrats to properly police this industry when they have received so many contributions from it?

_____

_____

_____

_____

_____

_____

_____

_____

_____

_____

_____

_____

_____

_____

_____

_____

_____

_____

For All Candidates

Q1: Do you support a nationwide data privacy law? If so, which specific provisions would it include?

Q2: Large tech companies are arguably bigger, more powerful, and more influential than basically any companies in history. Does this worry you, and should we do anything about it?

Q3: Do you believe that large tech companies like Apple, Google, Facebook, and Amazon should be broken up?

Q4: How do you plan to ensure as president that artificial intelligence is used ethically and in a way that safeguards the security and privacy of American citizens?

_____

_____

_____

_____

_____

_____

_____

_____

_____

_____

_____

_____

_____

★ 8 ★

THE AMERICAN DREAM

In 1931, a writer named James Truslow Adams wrote a book called *The Epic of America* in which he coined the term "The American Dream." He described its meaning as: "A land in which life should be better and richer and fuller for everyone, with opportunity for each according to ability or achievement."

Is the American Dream still alive? It depends whom you ask.

Twenty-three years after Adams published his book, another very different kind of book was published called *How to Lie with Statistics*. In it, the author showed how easy it was for someone to support their argument—and tell basically any story they wanted to tell—by selectively citing and shaping certain statistical measures.

Americans see this every day when politicians discuss the state of the American Dream. Ask President Trump and he'll tell you that "this is the greatest economy in the HISTORY of America." And he can point to data showing the unemployment rate dropping to 3.7% in October 2018, the lowest in almost 50 years. Ask Democratic presidential candidate Bernie Sanders and he'll decry America's "grotesque and growing level of wealth and income inequality." And he can point to data suggesting that the top earners in America have a greater share of national wealth and income than at any point since the 1920s.

President Trump and Sen. Sanders aren't lying about these numbers. They are just presenting the world as they want you to see it, namely that the American Dream is alive and well...or dead. But you can challenge President Trump's rosy employment narrative with data showing that many Americans have given up looking for work altogether and therefore aren't counted in the unemployment rate measure. And you can challenge Sen. Sanders's doom and gloom on income inequality by pointing out that the most commonly cited income inequality measures don't include the significant value Americans receive from tax benefits and other noncash assistance like government food and housing assistance.

Even statistics on the basic state and shape of the American middle class are up for dispute. Pessimists could say that the middle class is getting smaller, as only 32% of US families were considered middle class in 2014, compared to 37% in 1979. A more optimistic take would note that of the families who did leave the middle class during this same period, a higher percentage moved up to join the upper-middle class than those who descended to the lower-middle class or poverty.

We can play these number games all day.

Unsurprisingly, the American people appear as split on the state of the economy as our politicians are. Although a January 2019 Harvard-Harris poll had 66% of registered voters rating the US economy as "strong" or "somewhat strong," a separate question found 45% saying our economy is on the "right track," and 43% saying it's on the wrong track.

Both sides have a point.

THE ECONOMY IS ON...

THE RIGHT TRACK	THE WRONG TRACK
Job Market	
The unemployment rate hit a 49-year low of 3.7% in late 2018.	Rural America has been left behind. Ninety-nine percent of all job and population growth between 2008 and 2017 was concentrated in the 36% of US counties with a city that has a population over 50,000.
In late 2018 and early 2019, US wages grew at their fastest rate in a decade.	The average US salary has about the same purchasing power as it did 40 years ago.
A June 2018 Labor Department study found that there were more job openings than available workers to fill them.	Available jobs are often concentrated in certain industries and regions, and the share of Americans willing or able to move for a job has dropped by half.
In 2018, the number of women in the US workforce reached an all-time high.	For every unemployed American man between 25 and 55 years of age looking for work, there are three who are not looking at all.
Investment	
A record $293 billion in venture capital funding was invested in 2018.	Eighty percent of this funding went to just a few places: Silicon Valley and the Acela Corridor spanning Boston, New York City, and Washington, DC.
Education	
More than a third of Americans have a college bachelor's degree—the most ever.	Total student debt in the US is $1.52 trillion, or $37,712 for every student borrower.
Workforce Development	
The US spends $500 billion on higher education.	The US spends only $8 billion on worker training.
Wealth and Financial Security	
The stock market hit a record high in 2018.	Only 54% of US families own stocks.
The average nationwide 401(k) balance hit a new record high of $106,500 in 2018.	One in four nonretired adults has no retirement savings or pension.
According to the Federal Reserve, total US household wealth has almost doubled since the depths of the Great Recession.	Forty percent of American adults reported in a Federal Reserve Survey that if they were faced with an unexpected $400 expense, they would either not be able to pay it or would do so by selling something or borrowing money.

ANSWERS FROM THE LEFT AND RIGHT

The economic offerings from the Right and Left simply don't meet the current moment, but for different reasons:

- The Left's ideas to more fairly slice up the economic pie for some could shrink the pie for everyone.
- The Right's ideas to grow the pie do too little to ensure it is more fairly sliced.

THE LEFT: Government Will Take Care of It

The Left is stuck in 1965, the year Medicare passed. This period was the apex of big government liberalism, and a time when some on the Left imagined a large government program to solve every problem. In the 2020 election, the Left wants to push Democrats back to the future.

Virtually every new big economic idea from the Left entails a massive expansion of the government's role in the economy, even though 57% of the American public tells Pew Research Center they believe government is "almost always wasteful and inefficient." Among the Left's ideas:

- A federal jobs guarantee
- A federally mandated minimum wage
- Free or debt-free college
- Tax rates as high as 70%
- Corporate governance proposals that would enable Washington and outside interest groups to direct how and where private companies invest

In proposing a vast expansion of the public sector and significant new burdens on the private sector, the Left could threaten the engine of economic growth that generates the tax revenue upon which government depends.

Consider that in 2016, there were about 156 million jobs in America, of which about 22 million were with state, local, and federal governments. In other words, there are more than seven jobs in the private sector for everyone in the public sector. And yet, instead of nourishing the private sector, parts of the Left's economic agenda could decimate it.

THE RIGHT: You're on Your Own

If the Left is stuck in 1965, then the Right's economic philosophy often seems to be stuck in 1981. In short, the prescription is that whatever Ronald Reagan did…do more of it.

Although President Trump's more restrictive trade and immigration policies are very different from those offered by recent Republican leaders, his key economic policies have mostly followed the Reagan-era script of cutting regulations and cutting taxes.

The problem is that the core idea behind Reaganomics—that a rising tide of economic growth will lift all boats—is taking on water. In fact, for decades in the US and around the world, an increasing share of the economy's gains have been accruing to the people who own things at the expense of labor. Between 2000 and 2015, the share of corporate profits going to labor declined from 82.3% to 75.5%; the equivalent of $3,770 less for every worker.

President Trump sold his signature 2017 tax cut as a major boost for workers, but a late 2018 survey of 152 companies by the consultancy Korn Ferry found that most companies were not putting their tax savings toward increasing their payroll.

Lower taxes and less regulation—properly applied—can be good for the economy, but they are not a magic bullet. The nature of the American economy, and the challenges facing workers, has changed radically since 1981. But the Right's economic thinking has not.

SOLUTIONS:
THE NEW AMERICAN DREAM

As British Prime Minister Winston Churchill once remarked, "It has been said democracy is the worst form of government except for all those other forms that have been tried."

You could say much the same about capitalism, which despite its occasional failures, excesses, and inequities, has proven over time to unquestionably be the economic system that best encourages innovation and growth and enables people to meet their full potential. But capitalism can easily lose the support of a democratic citizenry if it isn't paired with a strong safety net capable of supporting people and communities that are inevitably left behind or face hardship when new industries and businesses are created and old ones are disrupted.

In 2018, a much-discussed poll found millennials had a more favorable opinion of socialism than they did capitalism. Millennials—and many others—are understandably frustrated that the economy isn't working well enough for them. But we don't think the answer to this frustration is for the next president to follow the Left's plan to radically restructure every sector of the economy with ideas that history has proven don't work. Nor should they assume strong GDP and corporate profits are sufficient—as the Right often does—to expand opportunities for American workers. Instead, they should pursue policies that support the many features that are working in the US economy but with a much more targeted focus on Americans who are unquestionably being left behind.

In 2018, scholars from the Brookings Institution and the American Enterprise Institute—among the most respected center-Left and center-Right think tanks in the country—released a comprehensive Work, Skills, Community Report to deal with many of the challenges we discuss in this chapter. Below we share a few of the policy prescriptions, from this report as well as ideas we unearthed elsewhere, that could be implemented at the federal level and that we think the next president should consider:

Bring Americans Back into the Workforce

While there should be support for Americans already looking for employment, we need to motivate those who could otherwise join the workforce to do so.

Expand the Earned Income Tax Credit

The earned income tax credit is a refundable tax credit (which means it can actually reduce someone's tax liability below zero) to ensure that working people receive a living wage. It is a more flexible and market-based approach to achieve a goal shared by many supporters of a national minimum wage, which is to bring dignity and security to working people everywhere. Expanding the size and eligibility of the earned income credit could be achieved by: expanding the number of families that pay estate taxes, limiting tax exemptions available to better-off households, or raising minimum taxes for corporations that rely on tax havens.

Wage Subsidy Pilot
Experiment with more direct ways to enhance the take-home pay of low-wage workers, inviting states and municipalities to propose pilot programs. Options could include worker tax credits or subsidies for each hour worked, which would take the form of money added to each paycheck alongside wages from employers.

Fix Unemployment Insurance
Strengthen incentives and expectations that recipients of unemployment insurance will seek new employment quickly. Provide lump-sum payments when claimants take a new job. Require them to pick up benefits at unemployment offices where they receive case management services. Lower thresholds for acceptable employment after prolonged job searches.

Fix Disability Insurance
During George H.W. Bush's presidency, only 2.5% of working-age Americans received disability checks from the Social Security Administration. The figure has now doubled to 5.2%. The federal government should rigorously review existing cases to determine whether beneficiaries are still disabled. Strengthen employer incentives to contest claims and accommodate workers with impairments rather than shift them to disability programs.

Financial Support for Long-Distance Moves
The federal government should expand the availability of financial support for individuals who want to make long-distance moves to places promising greater economic opportunity. At the same time,

federal policy should encourage states and localities to relax zoning restrictions and construct new housing units to increase the supply of affordable housing. For those who wish to stay in their communities to live but not necessarily to work, state and local governments could provide a subsidy for workers commuting to adjacent communities.

A Second Chance to Get Ahead

According to a *New York Times*/CBS News/Kaiser Family Foundation poll, men with criminal records account for about 34% of all non-working men ages 25–54. Give education and job training to people who have served time in prison so that they can provide for themselves and contribute to society. This could be achieved by mandating that previously incarcerated individuals participate in a reemployment program.

Train the Workforce of the Future

When a local factory moves offshore, national and local leaders are supposed to help workers land new jobs in different industries. But nearly across the board, retraining programs have failed to live up to their potential. Here are a few ways to improve training and education:

A Training Tax Credit

Create a federal tax credit modeled on the R&D tax credit to reimburse companies for 20% of new training offered to employees earning less than $60,000 a year.

Federal Financial Aid for Career Education

Provide federal financial aid for all career education that meets quality control standards, including short-term and nondegree programs at unaccredited institutions and options designed for older workers displaced by new technology.

Target Aid to the People Who Need It

Target federal financial aid to students who need it most, reallocating money currently spent on 529 education savings accounts, tuition tax credits, and graduate student loan forgiveness, all of which benefit primarily higher-income students.

Ease the Childcare Burden

One in five American families spends more than a quarter of their income on childcare. Below are a few ways to help working families:

Subsidized Family Leave

Subsidize eight weeks of paid parental leave, and encourage employers to offer up to 40 weeks of unpaid time.

Expanded Childcare Tax Credit

Make the child and dependent care tax credit more available to working-class families by making it refundable—payable to even families who do not earn enough to owe income taxes. Pay for the expansion by capping program eligibility at $80,000 per family per year. Strengthen state certification requirements for childcare programs.

Make Higher Education Affordable

The cost of attending a public four-year college has tripled in the last 30 years, and Washington is financing or facilitating more and more college loans. According to the Congressional Budget Office, the government financed roughly $100 billion in student loans and provided about $30 billion in grants and $30 billion in tax preferences in 2017.

Students bear most of the responsibility for repaying these loans while colleges often face little accountability for keeping costs down. In 2015 the Federal Reserve Bank of New York found that colleges raise tuition by 60 cents for every new dollar of subsidized loans they receive.

Ease the College Debt Burden

Increase the repayment period for US student loans from 10 years to 20–30 years and make repayment more contingent on a graduate's work situation, thus ensuring that repayments don't exceed a certain share of the graduate's income.

Make Colleges More Accountable for Reducing Costs

Recent studies have revealed that a growing share of colleges' budgets are going to administration instead of instruction, with the ranks of nonacademic and professional employees at colleges doubling in the last quarter century and vastly outpacing the growth of faculty or students.

It is time for a comprehensive overhaul of the federal student loan system, which would include colleges taking on more responsibility for keeping costs in control. One idea would be to require colleges to keep their tuition prices under the cost of inflation or risk having their students lose access to federal student loans.

Incentives for College Completion

Only 55% of Americans who go to college will get their degree within six years of enrolling. The federal government should:

- Provide new incentives for higher education institutions to focus on college completion as well as admission.
- Require public institutions of higher learning, and especially community colleges, to provide comprehensive student support services, including program and course advising, mentoring, and remedial education assistance for degree or certificate programs.
- Provide federal assistance through a block grant program to waive tuition for students enrolled in community colleges in these programs.

Give Workers a Fair Share

Research shows that companies with significant ownership by employees tend to grow faster, pay better, and are less likely to lay off employees during tough times. Federal laws and regulations should incentivize employers to give employees a greater stake in their employers' success. Frontline workers could, for example, receive a greater percentage of their income in stock (or have the stock granted in addition to their salary). Washington could provide tax incentives that credit companies a portion of the profits they distribute to employees beneath a certain cap.

Close the Skills Gap

Incentivize Degrees in High-Demand Fields

Too many Americans don't currently have the skills employers need. One way to fix this imbalance would be for the federal government to make more of its educational funding (e.g., Perkins loans) conditioned upon students pursuing majors in areas where there are projected future job shortages.

New Avenues for Worker Accreditation

College isn't right for everyone. The federal government could bring together stakeholders to create new types of accreditation beyond high school, college, and graduate school degrees to include accreditation (e.g., digital badges or microdegrees) that recognizes the acquisition of specific skills such as computer coding or leadership training.

Universal Computer Science Education

Make computer science courses available to every middle and high school student by 2020. Many local efforts and partnerships are underway to make this possible, but to bring computer education to every school, these bottom-up efforts will need top-down support from the federal government.

More Targeted Investment for Technical Education in K–12

Incorporate new courses such as computer programming, engineering, and data analytics into K–12 curricula to better prepare graduates for the workforce. The federal government can help by providing additional funding for STEM teacher training programs and creating STEM Innovation Networks by awarding grants to school districts in partnership with colleges to transform STEM education in K–12 schools.

Boost Small and New Businesses

According to the Kauffman Foundation, new businesses account for nearly all net new job creation in the US. The next president could clear the path for new business creation, especially in rural and disadvantaged areas, with the following ideas:

Regulatory Roadmap for Entrepreneurs

Small businesses are hit particularly hard by regulatory compliance, with regulations costing them over $10,000 per employee—36% higher than the cost to larger businesses. The federal government should develop a regulatory "roadmap" website that enables entrepreneurs to view all of the federal, state, and local regulations that may affect their business.

Expand Entrepreneurship by
Enhancing the Community Reinvestment Act

Minority-owned businesses have a tougher time getting access to credit and often pay higher interest rates. For example, loan denial rates for minority firms are about three times higher compared to those of nonminority-owned firms. Enhance the Community Reinvestment Act, which provides incentives for banks to meet the credit needs of people in low- and moderate-income neighborhoods, to allow more funding to be funneled to startup businesses.

Expand the Rural Business Investment Program

Rural businesses lack important access to financing since 80% of all venture capital investment goes to a few large metropolitan areas. An expansion of the Rural Business Investment Program, which helps create job opportunities in rural areas by meeting the equity capital investment needs of rural businesses, could help.

★2020★
CANDIDATE QUESTIONS

For President Trump

Q1: Forty percent of people say they can't handle an unexpected $400 expense without borrowing money or selling something. With so many people financially insecure, how can you claim the "economy is the greatest in American history?"

Q2: Workers are getting a lower share of national income and corporate profits than any time in the last 40 years. So my company is generally benefiting more from my work and I am getting less. What's your plan to fix it?

Q3: You said before the 2018 midterm elections that you were planning to push for a "major tax cut for middle-income people." But it doesn't look like middle-class tax cuts are moving through Congress now, and most of the studies of the tax cut you did sign show the majority of the benefits going to upper-income individuals. What's your plan to get more tax relief for middle-class people?

For Democratic Candidates

Q1: Unemployment is almost the lowest it has been in 50 years, and yet some people are saying we need Washington to pass a federal jobs guarantee. Do you agree?

- If yes, won't a bunch of people quit private sector jobs to work for the government? And how do you ensure these jobs are actually working on useful projects?

Q2: Do you think the federal government should pay for everyone to go to college? If so, why? Some people aren't cut out for college or don't want to go. Why should taxpayers foot this bill?

Q3: I see many candidates proposing federal "retraining programs for workers." But most of them don't really work. Why not, and what's your plan to fix them so people can actually get the training they need for the jobs that are available?

Q4: Do you believe that Congress should be able to limit companies' abilities to issue dividends and buy back shares?

- If so, why do you think Washington is better qualified to tell companies how and where to invest their money than the people who run and work at these companies?

For All Candidates

Q1: At least one quarter of current jobs in the US could be disrupted by automation. How do you plan to address the potential displacement of workers due to automation?

Q2: Only half of today's 30-year-old adults make more than their parents, whereas 90% of these adults in 1970 made more than their parents. What would you say to these young Americans who have lost faith in the American Dream?

Q3: The average student borrower has over $37,000 in college debt. What, if anything, do you think the federal government should do about this problem?

_____

_____

_____

_____

_____

_____

_____

_____

_____

_____

_____

_____

★ 9 ★

IMMIGRATION

If **ever there** were an issue where the Right and Left are living in parallel universes, it is immigration. Click on right-wing news, and you'll see story after story of illegal immigrants committing acts of violence and cruelty against innocent Americans. Click on left-wing news, and you'll see the opposite: story after story of the American government committing acts of cruelty against innocent immigrants. Between these two poles stand the vast majority of Americans, spectators in a fringe war that decidedly ignores their opinions.

Unlike the radicals on both sides, the vast center of the country has nuanced, considerate, and sensible views on how America should fix its antiquated immigration system. They believe immigrants are good for America, but they don't understand or agree with how or why the government lets people into our country. They want innocent people to be protected but also for our borders to be strong and our laws to be enforced.

Despite the rampant hysteria and vitriol in the immigration debate, most Americans are remarkably pragmatic about what is needed to fix our immigration system. It's a good thing, too, because everything about the immigration debate requires nuance. While both the Left and the Right tout their own curated facts and arguments, they rarely tell the whole story.

THE LEFT MIGHT HAVE A POINT...	BUT SO MIGHT THE RIGHT...
Illegal Immigration	
The number of illegal immigrants living in America has *effectively been flat* for the last ten years.	But the number of illegal immigrants in America also quadrupled in the two decades prior.
Crime	
Illegal immigrants *do* commit all categories of crime at lower rates than native-borns.	But unauthorized immigrants are also much more likely to be involved in fatal car accidents because they don't typically have driver's licenses.
Economic Impact	
Legal immigration *is* generally good for the economy and for US workers.	But it isn't good for all workers in all places, and the benefits accrue more to some (white-collar workers who live in cities) than others (blue-collar workers who don't).
The Character of America	
America *is and always has been* a nation that welcomes immigrants.	But the share of foreign-born people living in the US is now higher than at any point in almost a century.

The US needs a new approach to immigration: one that resolves the status of the unauthorized and creates a better process for selecting and tracking immigrant hopefuls.

Although illegal immigration dominates the public debate, the shape of America's system of legal immigration is just as consequential. How many people should receive the privilege of becoming Americans every year? Should family-based immigration continue to be the prime criterion for entry into the US, or should we give more weight to another, like the potential contributions of new arrivals to our economy?

What the American people want—and what Washington refuses to give them—is an immigration system that makes sense for the times we live in, provides security, and strengthens our country.

Fixing America's broken immigration system took on a new urgency in 2018 and 2019 when tens of thousands of migrants—many of them families with children fleeing violence in Central and Latin America—began showing up at the US border seeking asylum protection. The number of migrants seeking asylum protection in the US jumped 70% between 2017 and 2018 to 93,000, leading the head of US Customs and Border Protection to declare, "This increased flow presents, currently at our highest levels in over a decade, both a border security and humanitarian crisis."

Drug cartels and human traffickers are also exploiting this crisis, generating millions of dollars for their illegal activities by promising desperate families they can help get them to the US border. Although they'd never say it, it is hard to escape the conclusion that many of our leaders in Washington would rather campaign on the immigration issue than to actually solve it.

The last time Washington passed a comprehensive immigration reform bill was 54 years ago in 1965. In recent years, bipartisan immigration bills cleared the Senate twice by large margins (once in 2006, and once in 2013) but were left to die in the House because of the Speaker's refusal to allow a vote.

In the absence of Congress passing immigration reform, presidents have increasingly sought immigration fixes through unilateral executive action, as with President Obama's 2012 Deferred Action for Childhood Arrivals (DACA) program and President Trump's 2019 declaration of a national emergency to free up funding for a border wall. These types of actions aren't desirable or sustainable, and may not even be constitutional. The only long-term solution to America's immigration problem is bipartisan legislation passed in the Congress and signed by the president.

The American people are eager for an immigration deal forged in the center. It's time for the next president to deliver that deal.

HOW DOES OUR IMMIGRATION SYSTEM ACTUALLY WORK?

The United States is one of the few nations that puts an emphasis on family reunification in its immigration considerations. It leads the world in admitting immigrants due to family criteria, with 67% of those admitted in 2016 accepted for family-based reasons. Canada and Australia, on the other hand, place greater emphasis on economic factors.

JUSTIFICATIONS FOR ADMITTING NEW IMMIGRANTS

United States
- 67% - Family reunification
- 12% - Employment
- 21% - Other (incl. Humanitarian)

Canada
- 26.7% - Family based
- 31.5% - Employment
- 41.8% - Other (incl. Humanitarian)

Australia
- 27.7% - Family based
- 62.0% - Employment
- 10.3% - Other (incl. Humanitarian)

Immigration in the United States is governed through the Immigration and Nationality Act (INA), which provides several avenues through which people can enter the United States, including: family-sponsored, employment-based, diversity immigration (which gives preference to individuals of countries with low immigration to the US), and refugee and asylee status (for individuals fleeing war, violence, and political persecution).

Annually, the INA allows for a total worldwide cap of 675,000 immigrants, but this limit is often exceeded due to the unlimited nature of certain legal permanent resident categories. As a consequence, about one million immigrants arrive in the US each year.

In recent years, there has been an exponential increase in the number of people showing up at the US-Mexico border seeking asylum, which entitles people with this status to certain protections under US law. According to the American Immigration Council:

> Asylum is a protection granted to foreign nationals already in the United States or at the border who meet the international law definition of a "refugee." The United Nations 1951 Convention and 1967 Protocol define a refugee as a person who is unable or unwilling to return to his or her home country, and cannot obtain protection in that country, due to past persecution or a well-founded fear of being persecuted in the future "on account of race, religion, nationality, membership in a particular social group, or political opinion." Congress incorporated this definition into US immigration law in the Refugee Act of 1980.
>
> As a signatory to the 1967 Protocol, and through US immigration law, the United States has legal obligations to provide protection to those who qualify as refugees. The Refugee Act established two paths to obtain refugee status—either from abroad as a resettled refugee or in the United States as an asylum seeker.

In early 2019, in an effort to reduce the number of people seeking asylum in the US, President Trump signed a memorandum directing the US Justice Department and the Department of Homeland Security to develop several regulations that make it more difficult to claim asylum, including setting a fee for asylum applications.

Becoming a Citizen

Once individuals meet certain requirements—such as being a permanent resident for five years, being at least eighteen years old, and being able to read, write, and speak English—they can apply for naturalization (i.e., citizenship), a process that involves completing an interview, taking an exam, and submitting necessary documents, among other things.

ILLEGAL IMMIGRATION— WHAT'S REALLY HAPPENING

Most Americans believe illegal immigration is a significant problem. But it's hard to solve a problem when there's so much misinformation about what it looks like and why. Recent years have seen significant shifts in the number, nationality, and status of people living in the US illegally.

How Many are Coming?

The net number of illegal immigrants living in the US has not increased in the last ten years. In other words, the number of unauthorized immigrants entering the US equaled the number leaving.

- But illegal immigration exploded by a factor of 3.4 between 1990 and 2007: from 3,500,000 to 11,989,297.

Who Is Coming?

In the past few years, the nationalities of illegal immigrants shifted from almost exclusively Mexicans seeking work to more Latin and Central Americans seeking refuge from drugs and extreme violence at home.

- 2.5 million people were murdered in Latin America and the Caribbean between 2000 and 2017, almost three times the number of people killed combined in the armed conflicts in Iraq, Syria, and Afghanistan during the same period.
- Although Latin America is home to only 8% of the world's population, it is responsible for 33% of its homicides. Of the 20 countries in the world with the highest homicide rate, 17 are in Central and Latin America and the Caribbean.

The Border Might Not Be the Biggest Problem

In each of the last seven years, there were more illegal immigrants who came to the US legally but became illegal by overstaying their visas than there were unauthorized border crossers.

The Greatest Terror Threat Is Coming from...Canada?

In the first half of fiscal year 2018, only six illegal immigrants whose names were on the federal government's database of known or suspected terrorists were apprehended by Border Patrol at the US-Mexico border. During that same period, 41 individuals in the database were apprehended at the US-Canada border.

US Immigration Courts Are Overwhelmed

As of early 2019, there is a backlog of 850,000 cases in the US immigration court system with fewer than 500 judges available nationwide to handle them.

Illegal Immigration Is Concentrated in a Few Places

- Just six states account for 59% of all undocumented immigrants in the US.
- From 2010 to 2016, the immigrant populations in fifteen states grew by at least 15%.

THE IMPACT OF IMMIGRANTS ON THE ECONOMY, PUBLIC SAFETY, AND THE SOCIAL SAFETY NET

When it comes to immigration, there are three dominant questions on many Americans' minds:

- Does immigration increase or decrease the wages and economic prospects of native-born Americans?
- Does immigration make us more or less safe?
- Does immigration strain our social safety net?

The short answer to all three questions is: it depends. But there is plenty of research, conducted over several decades, that can provide credible insights on each.

Immigration Is Good for the US Economy

US economic growth is fueled by two key factors: either our workforce expands, or we become more productive—usually through technology that allows us to produce more with less. We are approaching trouble on both fronts.

Productivity has been slowing for decades, although Labor Department data from late 2018 and early 2019 showed worker productivity growing at the fastest rate in a decade. Still, innovation just isn't delivering the economic boost it once did. So America needs more people working to keep our economy growing, but the growth of the US labor force is slowing down for a simple reason: Baby boomers are retiring en masse, and our birth rate is now half what it was 50 years ago. Although President Trump memorably declared in early 2019 that "our country is full," the overall US population is actually growing at the slowest rate since the 1930s.

An orderly influx of legal immigrants could help solve this problem for the United States. Research shows that:

- Most immigrants enter the country young and work and pay taxes for decades.
- Immigrants are uniquely entrepreneurial, as they are twice as likely to start a business as native-born Americans. And some of these small businesses become very big businesses. More than half of all American startups worth $1 billion or more today were founded by immigrants, and several iconic US brands had immigrant founders including: Google, Pfizer, Chobani, Sara Lee, Nordstrom, DuPont, and Colgate.

But the benefits of immigration aren't shared equally. Some native-born American workers do worse—at least, in the short term.

- Immigration reduces the costs of goods for all Americans, with the most benefits accruing to white-collar workers who also benefit from lower costs for immigrant-heavy services like housekeeping and gardening.
- For less educated blue-collar workers, low-skilled (illegal) immigrants can reduce wages. Harvard researcher George Borjas found a 10% increase in low-skilled immigrants was associated with a wage drop for low-skilled Americans by 3%–4%.

Immigrants Do Not Make Us Less Safe Overall, but There's More to the Story

Both authorized and unauthorized immigrants are significantly less likely to be convicted of felonies and other crimes than are native-born Americans.

- After a careful analysis of Texas arrest records, the Cato Institute reported that illegal immigrants commit all categories of crime at lower rates than native-born Americans.

However, as with most issues regarding immigration, the topline numbers don't tell the whole story. Unlicensed drivers are almost five times more likely to be in a fatal crash than licensed ones. Only twelve states and DC allow unauthorized migrants to obtain driver's licenses, forcing many of them to drive without safety training. And of course, entering the United States illegally is itself a crime.

Legal Immigration Could Help Save Social Security

Immigrants—both high-skilled and low-skilled—have more children than native-born Americans and tend to enter the country as young adults.

- Making up just 13% of the US population, immigrants produced nearly 25% of births in 2015.

+ Because most immigrants enter the country at a young age, the chief actuary of Social Security estimates that immigration could add an additional $500 billion to Social Security's finances over the next 25 years and $4 trillion over the next 75.

Illegal Immigration Has Real Costs, Especially for Local Governments

Approximately $18.5 billion of medical care for unauthorized immigrants is publicly funded each year, with the heaviest burden falling on local health care systems.

+ In New York City, the largest public hospital system provides annual care to over 200,000 illegal immigrants each year at a cost of $400 million.
+ Sixty-five thousand illegal immigrants in Houston received care funded by charity.
+ California is expected to have around 1.5 million adult immigrant residents without insurance by 2019.

Some of these costs are offset by the $11.64 billion in state and local taxes undocumented immigrants pay each year. Illegal immigrants also contribute $7 billion to Social Security every year but never collect benefits due to their status.

WHY ARE BORDER SECURITY AND IMMIGRATION ENFORCEMENT SO DIFFICULT?

The United States has difficulty securing its southern border and keeping track of new immigrants once they arrive, despite investing $263 billion in border security since 1986 and having a slew of federal, state, and local agencies dedicated to regulating our borders and interior. Here are a few reasons why:

1. The US-Mexico Border—Where 98% of Border Apprehensions Occur—Is Huge

◆ Our border with Mexico is 1,933 miles long and spans Texas, Arizona, New Mexico, and California. As of 2015, only 703 miles of fencing have been installed.

◆ The terrain is difficult, and the border runs through water, mountains, Native American and private land, and a national park.

2. Border and Internal Enforcement Is a Bureaucratic Mess

◆ Authorities don't have the right infrastructure or technology to share information and intelligence.

◆ Coordination is lacking among federal, state, and local authorities. Enforcing immigration policy requires different levels of government to collaborate on identification, detention, and deportation. It often does not happen. And individual states such as Vermont, California, and the District of Columbia have enacted legislation in support of sanctuary policies that prohibit information sharing with local and government officials.

☆ THE COST OF A BORDER WALL ☆

While costs can vary wildly, the accepted budget for President Trump's border wall—meant to cover the remaining unfortified gaps of land—ranges between $15 and $25 billion. Some suggest more cost-effective alternatives like video surveillance, aerial monitoring, and sensors, and its implementation along the same area as President Trump's proposed wall would cost only $145 million.

THE DREAMERS

The fate of Dreamers—young people brought to America illegally by their parents—is one of the most contentious elements of the immigration debate. At issue is Deferred Action for Childhood Arrivals (DACA), a program instituted through executive order by President Obama in 2012. It provided eligible grantees deferred action on deportation for two years with the option to renew, as well as eligibility for a work permit, Social Security card, and driver's license. Out of 1.9 million individuals who are eligible for DACA, about 800,000 are currently protected under the program.

Here are a few statistics about Dreamers:

♦ On average, Dreamers came to America when they were six years old.
♦ 97% of them are working or in school.
♦ Nine hundred of them are serving in the US military.

On September 5, 2017, then Attorney General Jeff Sessions announced that the Trump administration was ending DACA in an attempt to force Congress to pass a long-term solution. A congressional solution has still not been passed, and Dreamers remain in limbo.

ANSWERS FROM THE LEFT AND RIGHT

Of late, neither the far Left nor the far Right has much interest in a real immigration debate or a comprehensive solution. Instead, what they offer is political symbolism used to fire up their bases—along with half-baked measures that would treat only the symptoms of broader immigration problems.

One of, if not the most fundamental problems in the US immigration system is the lack of coordination between the federal government and state and local officials. And yet what the Left and the Right have recently suggested would inarguably make this even worse.

THE LEFT: **Abolish ICE**

Too many on the Left are quick to accuse security-concerned Americans of racism and xenophobia and to dismiss the potential dangers of unregulated immigrant flows. Of late, "Abolish ICE" has become a rallying cry for the Left. In a 2018 *Politico* poll, just 25% of Americans agreed that the federal government should eliminate ICE.

THE RIGHT: **Close Our Borders**

Too many on the Right seem increasingly mean-spirited, proposing draconian cuts to even legal immigration, lengthy jail sentences for unauthorized border crossers, and even the refusal of emergency medical care for those living illegally in the US.

The Trump administration's policy to separate families crossing the border—and to hold parents and children separately while they awaited trial—was opposed by two-thirds of the American public, according to several polls taken in 2018. This policy was later reversed under strong public pressure.

SOLUTIONS:
HIGH WALL, BIG GATE

This phrase was coined by the *New York Times* columnist Tom Friedman, and it accurately describes both the political and policy imperatives for any immigration deal forged in the center.

"High Wall" doesn't mean we literally need to build a huge wall on the southern border, though more physical barriers are certainly necessary in some places. It does mean the American people want their leaders to get serious about securing our border and getting a handle on who is coming into the country. "Big Gate" means all Americans will benefit from our remaining an open and welcoming country that attracts talented, freedom-seeking people from around the world.

Immigration is an issue that is difficult to solve piecemeal, for reasons of both policy and politics. Immigration is a system with many policy parts—tweak one part and you will inevitably impact several others. As for the politics, any immigration deal will inevitably require leaders on both sides to both give and to get, in a way that will drive their respective bases on the Left and Right crazy. Leaders will be more likely to take this risk if they have a big pool of policy bargaining chips that could allow each side to walk away from the negotiating table with policy wins.

♦ 63% of registered voters favor a congressional deal that gives undocumented immigrants brought here by their parents work permits and a path to citizenship in exchange for increasing merit preference over preference for relatives, eliminating the diversity visa lottery, and funding barrier security on the US-Mexico border. (*June 2018 Harvard-Harris poll*)

So, although many of these reforms listed below would be welcome on their own, we have also combined these solutions as a potential cohesive package that is designed to meet both the policy and political imperatives of our current moment. The next president could forge an immigration deal in the center with six key features.

1. Shift Toward More Employment-Based Immigration

The US currently admits almost five times as many immigrants for family-based reasons as employment-related ones. We should shift our targets closer to those from countries like Canada, which currently has an almost equal split. Like Canada, the US could use a points system to determine which immigrants qualify for employment-related entry, with criteria including:

♦ Education, with the most points given for a PhD or equivalent
♦ English language ability
♦ Work experience
♦ Age, with the highest points going to those between the ages of 21 and 49

- Arranged employment (those who already have job offers)
- Adaptability, which includes previous work experience in the United States or a family connection to make assimilation easier

Other significant legal immigration reforms should include:

- *Eliminating the Diversity Immigrant Lottery* in favor of immigrants who possess functional English language skills, have achieved superior education or employment experience, or have American family members.
- *Fixing the Asylum System* by creating clearer standards for who can qualify.
- *Addressing the Immigration Case Backlog* by continuing to increase the hiring of immigration judges.
- *Limiting Family-Related Immigration to Nuclear Families* specifically to spouses, minor children, and parents of US citizens and the spouses and minor children of legal permanent residents.
- *Prioritizing the Best Applicants, Regardless of Origin:* Allow the number of legal immigrants admitted to stay roughly the same while eliminating per-country immigration limits to allow for the admission of the best-qualified applicants.

    - 70% of Americans call for immigration levels to be kept the same (38%) or increased (32%). (June 2018 Pew Research poll)

- *Having Foreign Workers Pay to Train American Workers*: A new nonprofit, IDEAL Immigration, has a novel proposal—to both deal with the shortage of qualified workers in various jobs and industries and to improve the skills of US workers—called the Workforce Visa Act, which would include the following features:

    1. Creates a one-year renewable visa (W-Visa) for foreign workers who have a job offer and pay $2,500 to a federal workforce development fund.

2. In order to employ workers, companies would have to pay an extra $2,500 annually—in addition to wages—to reimburse the worker for their contribution to the workforce development fund. These payments—from the foreign worker to the workforce development fund and the subsequent reimbursement from the company to the worker—would be made each year in which the foreign worker is employed and will help ensure no employer has an incentive to hire an immigrant over an equally qualified US citizen.

3. The Workforce Development Trust Fund would disperse billions of dollars in fees to states (based on how many workers each state receives) in order to fund state workforce development programs.

4. As an incentive not to overstay and comply with the rules, the foreign workers could apply for legal permanent residence after ten renewals if they pay an additional $25,000 to the workforce development fund.

5. Workers are ineligible for any government benefits until becoming permanent residents, and years they spend working prior to achieving permanent residency would not accrue toward any future Social Security benefits.

2. Get the Undocumented out of the Shadows

It is unacceptable to have over 11 million people living illegally in America. But mass deportation is unacceptable too—both morally and logistically. Unauthorized immigrants living in the US should be brought out of the shadows and offered a long and rigorous road toward citizenship that depends on them maintaining clean criminal records, paying taxes, and meeting several other requirements.

- ◆ 64% of Americans say immigrants living in the country illegally should have a chance to become legalized so long as they meet certain requirements. *(2017 PRRI poll)*

3. Build a Wall Where It Works

It is essential to have a fortified border that allows the US to reliably and consistently prevent unauthorized entry. For example, the Rio Grande Valley Sector in Texas saw more than half of all US-Mexico family unit border apprehensions. In addition to the fencing scheduled to be built in the area, more funding should be designated to fill uncovered spots.

Other parts of the border make a physical barrier impractical, where more border security personnel, drones, and other surveillance could fill the gap. These border fortification measures should be coupled with revised legal measures that quicken deportation proceedings to deter crossings.

- 61% of registered voters believe US border security is inadequate. *(June 2018 Harvard-Harris poll)*

4. Get Serious about Internal Immigration Enforcement

Immigration enforcement needs to refocus on unauthorized individuals who conduct criminal activity in the US. And employers need to step up to play a lead role in preventing illegal immigration. To improve internal immigration enforcement, the federal government needs to:

- ***Require a Universal E-Verify System*** that would assist employers in ensuring that they only employ individuals who are authorized to work in the United States. Potential employers have an essential role to play in enforcement. If undocumented immigrants can't work, many will return home. E-Verify technology has significantly improved in recent years in its ability to limit false negatives and positives.

  - 79% of Americans support requiring employers to verify all new employees are living in the US legally. *(September 2017 Washington Post-ABC News poll)*

- *Get Serious About Visa Overstays*: Biometric technologies (which use methods like fingerprints and facial recognition) have advanced significantly in recent years. A robust and fully funded biometric entry and exit system—which would include regular text and email communications to visa holders from the Department of Homeland Security alerting them to departure deadlines —should be implemented immediately.

Illegal immigration detention has to be humane, which means we should:

- *Establish a Legal Mechanism for Enforcing Higher Civil Detention Standards in ICE Detention Centers*, and allow for more frequent inspections that increase both accountability and transparency.
- *Discontinue the Use of Private Prisons and County Jails for Immigrant Detention*, thus reducing the financial corner-cutting that causes deaths, suicides, sexual abuse, and lack of access to medical care.
- *End Mandatory Detention*: Ensure that individuals are not placed in detention centers unless they are deemed a threat to the public or a flight risk.

5. Address the Source of the Asylum Problem

In early 2019, President Trump threatened to suspend as much as $450 million in US foreign aid to Guatemala, Honduras, and El Salvador, claiming their governments were not doing enough to prevent their citizens from heading northward for the US border, with many seeking asylum. (As of this writing, the aid funding has not been withdrawn.) While the president's frustration is understandable, suspending this aid would almost certainly worsen the economic and security conditions in these countries and compel even more people to flee the desperation in their homelands.

According to James Stavridis, the former commander of the United States Southern Command, "Suddenly stopping all foreign aid…will only increase the driving forces creating the caravans over time, which will be even more costly to deal with on our border. It is like stopping your preventative medications, then wondering why your disease has spread a year later."

Instead of suspending foreign aid to these troubled countries, the US should increase it, as there is strong evidence that the US Agency for International Development (USAID) programs in Latin America are helping to significantly reduce violence in some communities.

6. Let the Kids Stay

Dreamers should not be held culpable for the actions of their parents, who brought them to the US. If they contribute to American society and the economy by working, acquiring an education, or serving in the military, then they should have access to a path to citizenship assuming clean criminal records.

- ◆ 73% of Americans support allowing Dreamers to become citizens so long as they don't have a criminal record. *(February 2018 Monmouth University poll)*

★2020★
CANDIDATE QUESTIONS

For President Trump

Q1: In your 2019 State of the Union, you said you wanted to admit legal immigrants into the US in the "largest numbers ever." But your administration has pushed several policies to make legal immigration harder. Can you explain this disconnect?

Q2: In 2018, Senate Democrats offered you $25 billion for a border wall in exchange for giving the Dreamers a path to citizenship. In the deal you struck with Congress in early 2019, you got barely a billion dollars. Why didn't you take the deal that would have gotten $25 billion for the wall, and would you take a similar deal today?

Q3: Aside from building a border wall, what is the single most important policy change you want to see made to our immigration system?

Q4: A lot of police chiefs say they don't want to make their departments extensions of ICE because it harms the trust their officers need to build to police their communities. What do you say to that?

For Democratic Candidates

Q1: Do you support abolishing ICE? If you do, how exactly would you propose doing it? And if not, how would you propose reforming it?

Q2: Democrats have never liked the idea of President Trump's wall. But in 2018, 45 Senate Democrats were willing to give President Trump $25 billion for a border wall in exchange for a path to citizenship for the Dreamers. By early 2019, Democratic leaders like House Speaker Nancy Pelosi were calling the wall "immoral." Isn't this a pretty clear example of Democrats being hypocritical and politicizing the issue?

Q3: Too much immigration too fast is clearly harming the stability of some countries in Europe. Are you worried about that happening here?

_____

_____

_____

_____

_____

_____

_____

_____

_____

_____

For All Candidates

Q1: What's one big thing that you think many in your party are wrong about when it comes to immigration?

Q2: Immigration and asylum requests are increasing around the world due to political unrest. What can we do for countries to help them be less corrupt and more politically stable so people don't have to flee?

Q3: What are your three top priorities in terms of how you want to reform our immigration system?

_____

_____

_____

_____

_____

_____

_____

_____

_____

_____

_____

_____

★ 10 ★

THE MAGIC
MONEY TREE

n 2017, then British Prime Minister Theresa May appeared on BBC's *Question Time* when a nurse from the country's National Health Service said that her salary had barely budged at all in the last eight years. The nurse asked, "How can that be fair, in light of the job that we do?"

The prime minister responded by talking about the "hard choices" government had to make and then closed with a comment that was as colorful as it was controversial: "There isn't a magic money tree that we can shake that suddenly provides for everything that people want."

Politically, May's response was a disaster; it sounded condescending, tone-deaf, and dismissive of the concerns of a hard-working nurse. But May's money tree quote perfectly describes how both President Trump and the Democratic presidential candidates apparently plan to deal with America's budget problem which can be summarized as follows:

* The US government now annually spends almost $1 trillion more than it receives from tax revenues.

Leaders in both parties apparently think we can just shake the magic money tree to pay for new priorities and pay off our debts. Neither President Trump nor the Democratic contenders have realistic proposals to make a measurable impact on our deficit (the difference between what the government spends and receives in taxes each year) or our debt (the cumulative total of all our past annual deficits). In fact, as you will read later in this chapter, the Right and Left increasingly rely on obscure, untested, or flawed economic theories to suggest that maybe deficits don't really matter after all.

The presidential candidates aren't paying a price for failing to reckon with the debt because the American people seem less concerned about it than ever before. According to a 2019 Pew Research Center poll, just 48% of Americans say the "budget deficit should be a top priority for the president and Congress," which is 24 points lower than the 72% of Americans who answered the same question in the affirmative just five years ago.

It's hard to blame them. Deficit alarmists have been warning for years that America would pay for its profligate ways; that we'd wake up one day and find ourselves in the same situation Greece did in 2010, with creditors refusing to buy our debt, interest rates soaring, and our economy collapsing. And yet here we are in 2019 with a robust economy and interest rates at historic lows, which means rates for mortgage and car loans are too.

But this doesn't mean the deficit hawks are wrong. It may just mean they are early. The debt is a growing problem that could become a crisis if the next president doesn't take it seriously. Even so, we have no illusions about how difficult it will be to get 2020 presidential candidates to talk seriously about the debt.

Talking about the debt doesn't usually win candidates many votes. In 1984, Democratic presidential candidate Walter Mondale thought he was being a straight shooter about our budget challenges when he famously said: "Mr. Reagan will raise taxes, and so will I. He won't tell you. I just did."

Mondale lost 49 of 50 states to Reagan in that November's election.

In the 1992 election, Ross Perot had his scary debt pie charts and bar graphs. He lost every state.

Tackling the deficit may not be a winning message for 2020 either. But that doesn't mean the American people should let candidates get away with skirting the issue.

THE PROBLEM:
DEBT HELD BY THE PUBLIC IS $16.1 TRILLION AS OF DECEMBER 31, 2018*

- ◆ Annual federal deficit could reach $1 trillion by the end of 2019.
- ◆ Interest payments alone on US national debt are projected to reach $390 billion this year. That's almost one quarter of all the income taxes the government took in last year and more than 60% of the entire budget of the Department of Defense.

Putting the Debt in Context

Politicians sometimes like to compare the national debt to a family's household budget. They will say government is "maxing out our nation's credit card," or that it needs to "tighten its belt" just like families do. This is the wrong way to think about it.

The federal government is nothing like a household, beginning with the fact that it can print its own currency. The United States also has the added benefit of being the world's reserve currency, which means much of the world does business in US dollars. When recessions hit, investors the world over funnel money into US Treasury bonds because they view it as the world's safest asset. This helps keeps interest rates low for US consumers. There are also times—like during a recession—when it is responsible for a government to run deficits to help stimulate employment and economic activity.

---

* You may read elsewhere that America's national debt is over $22 trillion. But this figure is inclusive of "intragovernmental debt," which is debt the US Treasury owes to other federal agencies. Most funds are owed to retiree programs such as Social Security and federal and military pensions. We use the $15.8 billion "debt help by the public" figure as our benchmark in this chapter because that's the one that most economists consider most relevant as a measure of a country's financial health.

FEDERAL DEBT HELD BY THE PUBLIC
% of GDP

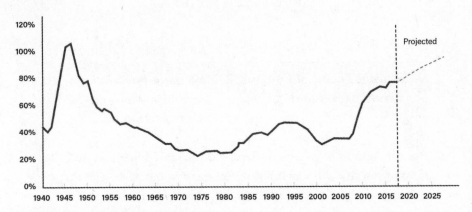

Source: CBO, 2018

But what is completely irresponsible is what America is doing right now, which is running nearly $1 trillion annual deficits when the economy is growing and the unemployment rate is almost at a 50-year low. In the near future, if the economy slows and Washington continues to do nothing about our budget problems, the annual deficit could reach as high as $2 trillion.

As big as these deficit and debt numbers are, they ultimately aren't the most important measure of America's fiscal health. What really matters is our public debt as a share of our total economy (debt/GDP). Governments can responsibly run annual deficits so long as their economy is growing fast enough to outpace the increasing debt. But when the public debt/GDP ratio gets too high, it suggests the government is headed for trouble.

And the US is headed for trouble. America's debt/GDP is now higher as a share of our economy than at almost any time since World War II.

In fact, according to a recent report from the International Monetary Fund, the United States is the only advanced economy in the world projected to increase its debt/GDP over the next five years.

UNITED STATES STANDS OUT

Change in Debt-to-GDP Ratio, 2018-2023

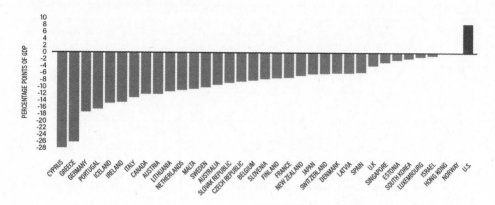

WHAT IS CAUSING THE PROBLEM?

Next time you hear a politician or a presidential candidate say their plan to tackle the deficit is to get rid of "waste, fraud, and abuse," you should translate it in your head into its true meaning: "I don't really have a plan."

Let's be clear: waste, fraud, and abuse is a problem in government at every level. And every president should seek to reduce or eliminate it. But getting rid of it is hard, and antiwaste and fraud measures often recover just a few billion dollars—not much in the context of a $4.1 trillion federal budget.

Politicians also love to suggest slashing certain kinds of federal spending that (1) don't have much political support and/or (2) represent a rounding error in the federal budget. A classic example is foreign aid. Americans wildly overestimate how much the US spends in this area, with the average respondent in a recent Kaiser Family Foundation survey guessing that 26% of all US federal spending went to foreign assistance. The real figure is less than one percent.

Americans might imagine that government wastes most of our tax money on useless programs and things they don't like. But the biggest drivers of our national debt are things Americans like the most:

- ◆ Entitlement programs like Social Security and Medicare
- ◆ Tax cuts

What Is Really Driving the Debt?

Spending

Americans are accustomed to regular government shutdowns, which are often caused by Congress's inability to agree on how or where money should be spent in the federal budget. But you might be surprised to learn that these increasingly contentious budget debates focus on only 31% of all federal spending. The other 69% is basically on autopilot, and it keeps growing every year.

WASHINGTON'S TWO KINDS OF SPENDING	
Mandatory Spending	Discretionary Spending
The 69% share includes programs like Social Security, Medicare, and interest payments on the debt, and refers to ongoing obligations the government is legally required to pay every year.	The 31% share must be "appropriated" each year, and includes everything else that Congress fights over when trying to pass a budget.
Mandatory spending typically goes to fund consumption in the present.	Discretionary spending often represents investments in the future, as funding for priorities like medical research, education, and infrastructure plant the seeds for future economic growth.

Fifty years ago, the federal government spent twice as much on discretionary (future-oriented) spending as it did mandatory. Now, the ratio is flipped, with government spending twice as much on mandatory as discretionary spending. And this disparity will keep growing over time.

As for Social Security and Medicare—the two programs most responsible for the growth in mandatory spending—their finances become more tenuous every year. In early 2019, the annual report from the program's trustees forecast that under current law, Social Security will be unable to fully pay promised benefits by 2035 and that Medicare will be unable to do the same by 2026.

Mandatory programs and interest costs will take over more of the federal budget, squeezing discretionary programs

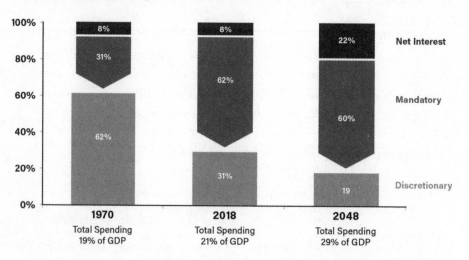

Source: Office of Management and Budget, Budget of the United States Government, Fiscal Year 2019, February 2018; and Congressional Budget Office, The 2018 Long-Term Budget Outlook, June 2018. Calculated by Peter G. Peterson Foundation.
Note: Numbers may not sum to totals due to rounding. Mandatory programs include Social Security, major federal health programs, other entitlement programs and offsetting receipts.

Taxation

President Trump's 2017 tax cuts did have beneficial impacts for the economy, including providing a short-term boost to economic growth and corporate profits even as it failed to deliver the large wage gains that were expected for workers. Throughout 2018, growth in the US was much stronger than in other developed economies around the world.

But tax cut supporters made an even more ambitious promise: that it would also reduce the deficit. According to President Trump's Treasury Secretary Steve Mnuchin, the tax plan would "not only pay for itself but in fact create additional revenue for the government."

He was wrong. Last year's federal deficit was $200 billion higher than it would have been without the tax cuts, and the Congressional Budget Office (CBO) recently estimated that the law will add $1.9 trillion to the national debt through 2027.

When and How the Debt Becomes a Problem

As we noted earlier, analogies between household and government finances usually don't make sense. But there is at least one instance in which it does.

If you apply for a mortgage—but have bad credit—the bank will typically charge you a higher interest rate to compensate for the risk you might not pay back the loan.

Investors in government debt think much the same way. Fortunately, the United States, over 200-plus years, has built a reputation that we always pay our bills. As a consequence, investors—in America and around the world—have had confidence they'll always get their money back with interest if they lend money to the US Treasury.

If and when that sentiment changes, we have a problem. As No Labels cofounder Andrew Tisch wrote in a 2017 op-ed:

> If a moment arrives when people don't think the US will repay its debts, investors will demand a higher risk premium in the form of higher interest rates. And the costs would be massive.
>
> Earlier this month, the interest rate on Illinois state debt spiked 80 basis points (0.8%) amid the state's ongoing budget crisis and the threat of a ratings agency downgrade.
>
> If the interest rate on US Treasuries spiked the same amount…it would increase the federal government's annual interest payments by over $100 billion, while making every consumer product with an interest rate—from car and credit card loans to mortgages—more expensive.

Deficit Reduction Ideas That Don't Reduce the Deficit

Politicians in Washington are fond of several symbolic gestures that make it appear as if they care about the deficit but usually amount to nothing. Among them:

1. The Debt Ceiling

As failed policies go, they don't get much worse than the debt ceiling, which creates a legal limit on how much debt the US Treasury Department can issue. The debt ceiling, which has existed since 1917, has utterly failed to keep the national debt in check.

As Tisch wrote in the same 2017 op-ed: "An idea like the debt ceiling could only be cooked up in Washington; instead of restraining Congress from spending taxpayer money, it invites them to run up debt first and then debate later whether to pay for it—or not."

The debt ceiling sounds fiscally responsible. But it's dangerously irresponsible. Congressional votes to raise the debt limit are frequently accompanied by grandstanding members of Congress threatening not to vote for it unless they can squeeze out a favored policy concession like spending cuts. If Congress ever failed to raise the debt limit, it would destroy America's reputation as a country that always pays its bills.

And we'd all pay the price.

2. Balanced Budget Amendment

Members of Congress—mostly on the Right—periodically push for a balanced budget amendment that would require federal revenues and expenditures to be balanced each year. But this is bad economic policy; sometimes, like during recessions, the government should run a deficit, and balanced budget amendments only apply to the discretionary part of the budget that makes up less than a third of all federal spending.

Lately, members of Congress have voted for huge deficit-financed spending increases and tax cuts only to then tout their support for a balanced budget amendment. Former Sen. Alan Simpson (R-WY)—who was cochair of the 2010 Simpson-Bowles Deficit Reduction Commission—calls this "chest-pounding fakery."

3. PAYGO

"PAYGO" rules come in different forms but typically require any tax cut or spending increase passed by Congress to be offset by tax increases or spending cuts elsewhere in the budget. As with the balanced budget amendment, PAYGO only applies to the small discretionary part of the budget, and it could force lawmakers into arbitrary or harmful spending cuts during recessions or artificially limit beneficial spending (for priorities like infrastructure) that could boost economic growth and employment.

ANSWERS FROM THE LEFT AND RIGHT

During the 1980 Republican presidential primary, then candidate George H.W. Bush famously described Ronald Reagan's economic agenda as "voodoo economics."

The line didn't work well politically (Bush lost the primary), and Reagan would go on to oversee strong economic and job growth during his eight years as president. But the late Bush's catchphrase has new relevance today because both the Right and the Left—instead of offering solutions to deal with the debt—have their own versions of voodoo economics that conveniently give them excuses to lower taxes or increase spending without having to reckon with any of the corresponding trade-offs.

THE LEFT: Print More Money

On the Left, a relatively obscure academic idea called "modern monetary theory" (MMT) is now being used to justify massive increases in federal spending. The gist of the idea is that governments—because they control their own currency—can pay off deficits merely by printing more money. If this spurred inflation, MMT adherents suggest that Congress could raise taxes—which would take money out of the system and theoretically stabilize the economy.

"Theoretically" is the key word. MMT is untested. And it makes the stability of the economy dependent on the willingness of Congress to take the politically difficult step of raising taxes right as the economy—and inflation—is heating up. That's a pretty shaky foundation to build our economy on.

Federal Reserve Chairman Jerome Powell, testifying to Congress in early 2019, said, "The idea that deficits don't matter for countries that can borrow in their own currency, I think, is just wrong."

THE RIGHT: Tax Cuts!

The Right has a view on taxes that starts with a sensible premise: Lower taxes are good for the economy because when you tax work and investment less, you will generally get more of both. But the Right has increasingly taken this idea to the extreme, suggesting that tax cuts are always the solution to our economic problems, including reducing the deficit. They claim that tax cuts will spur so much economic growth—and result in higher tax revenues—that they will effectively pay for themselves. But a variety of studies have shown that tax cuts pay for no more than a third of their initial cost, and other studies peg the figure at much less. There is not—and never has been—any free lunch in economics. Tax cuts are no different.

SOLUTIONS:
A REAL PLAN

Force Congress to the Table

In 2010, the bipartisan Simpson-Bowles Deficit Reduction Commission produced a report laying out a long-term vision to stabilize America's finances through a mix of modest and gradual spending cuts and tax increases.

The report was sensible, responsible…and dead on arrival. Members of Congress from both parties could not distance themselves from Simpson-Bowles fast enough.

Politicians are smart enough to know that most policy ideas—especially most deficit reduction ideas—never become law. And they didn't want to go on the record to support the kinds of tax increases or spending cuts that give opponents easy fodder for attack ads. Washington can't and won't solve the deficit issue unless our leaders are forced to the table by a crisis or a mechanism that simply will not let them kick the deficit can down the road any longer.

This is not an impossible challenge. Getting America's finances in order does not mean that the government's revenues and expenses must be in complete balance every year. It does mean the trajectory of our budget needs to change. Small changes to revenue and spending implemented and phased in now can make a significant difference over time.

There are a few ideas the next president could embrace to force Washington to confront the looming debt challenge.

A Fiscal Responsibility Act

The next president should support the implementation of a public debt/GDP limit that could only be violated with a formal Declaration of War or a supermajority vote of both houses of Congress and the signature of the president. This new public debt/GDP limit would replace the current debt ceiling limit and the debt ceiling limit would be repealed.

America's current public debt/GDP ratio is about 78%. The Fiscal Responsibility Act could prevent that ratio from exceeding 100%.

This proposal does not tell Congress how to get our fiscal house in order, and it does not require members to go on the record to support specific budget cuts and revenue increases. It does, however, require Congress to better align spending and revenues over an appropriate period of time. Absent a mechanism like the Fiscal Responsibility Act, the most likely course of action is for our federal debt to continue growing exponentially.

Fix the Budget Process

The most basic responsibility Congress has is deciding how much money the government takes in and how much it spends.

It's been clear for a long time Congress does not take this responsibility seriously. In fact, Congress has only passed its annual budget and spending bills on time four times in the last four decades, and not at all since 1997. The upshot is more wasteful and inefficient government. When Congress fails to pass spending bills on time, it relies on temporary spending measures called continuing resolutions—which typically provide the money federal agencies need to operate based roughly on what they spent the previous year.

What continuing resolutions don't provide is any chance for Congress to debate the most fundamental question of all: Why are we spending this money? Congress spends first and asks questions later when it should instead be spending only after figuring out which goals it hopes to achieve.

Meanwhile, Congress's constant stop-and-go budgeting creates havoc for government agencies and the citizens who depend on them. The following three ideas could help improve the current slapdash budget process.

No Budget, No Pay

If Congress can't make spending and budget decisions on time, its members shouldn't get paid on time either. Every government fiscal year begins October 1. If the congressional appropriations (spending) process does not conclude by that date, congressional pay would cease as of October 1 and would not be restored until appropriations were completed. Under "No Budget, No Pay," members of Congress would not receive any back pay lost as a consequence of their budget tardiness.

Biennial Budgeting

Congress should establish a two-year "biennial" budgeting cycle for the US government, which would enable members to focus more on long-term strategic planning. Under this new biennial budgeting process, Congress would complete its budget resolution and appropriations bills in the first year of each Congress and conduct an oversight and review process in the second year to evaluate which programs are and are not working.

Annual Fiscal Report

One of the chief obstacles to fixing America's finances is that no one agrees what's really on our balance sheet. When leaders in Washington debate our budget, they routinely use different baselines, projections, and assumptions, which often conveniently support whichever policy they are pushing at the moment. To quote an old Scottish writer, many of Washington's leaders "use statistics as a drunken man uses lamp posts—for support rather than for illumination."

But the problem is worse than just elected leaders cherry-picking their favorite numbers off the US government's balance sheet. It is the fact that the balance sheet itself is not reliable or accurate. Look no further than this shocking excerpt from a 2018 blog post from the US Government Accountability Office (GAO):

> As in past years, we were unable to render an audit opinion—i.e., a conclusion on whether the financial information is reliable—on the government's FY18 consolidated financial statements. Many of the same deficiencies that have affected past financial statements continue to get in the way of the government having reliable, useful, and timely financial information, including:
>
> * Problems with the Department of Defense's financial management and auditability;
> * The federal government's inability to adequately account for certain transactions between agencies; and
> * Weaknesses in the process for preparing the consolidated financial statements.
>
> In addition to these impediments, we identified other material weaknesses in controls over financial reporting—problems that could lead to significant errors in the consolidated financial statements—including:
>
> * The federal government's improper payments problem, which grew to an estimated $151 billion for FY18;
> * Information security across government; and
> * Loans receivable and loan guarantees liabilities.

According to the Securities and Exchange Commission, every public company in America is required to file regular financial statements that an independent auditor determines to be "accurate, truthful, and complete." And yet the federal government—the largest organization in the country, with a $4 trillion annual budget—apparently can't meet the same standard according to its own auditor.

The American people deserve to know what's really happening with our nation's finances, and the next president and Congress should at least be able to work off the same set of numbers. In addition to passing new legislation to strengthen the audit requirements of federal agencies, every year, a nonpartisan leader such as the comptroller general should deliver a televised fiscal update in person to a joint session of Congress. The president, vice president, all cabinet members, senators, and members of Congress should be required to attend this fiscal update session. They should be required to take individual responsibility for the accuracy and completeness of the comptroller general's report by signing the report, just as CEOs are required to affirm the accuracy of their companies' financial reporting.

★2020★
CANDIDATE QUESTIONS

For President Trump

Q1: When you were running for president in 2016, you said you were the "king of debt" and that you "loved debt." America's annual deficit is now almost $1 trillion. Why haven't you done more to get our finances in order?

Q2: Last year, you asked all of your cabinet secretaries to cut their agencies' budgets by 5%. But excluding the Department of Defense—for which you are increasing spending—federal agencies make up only 16% of the entire budget. Do you have a plan to deal with the big drivers of our debt, which are programs like Medicare and Social Security?

Q3: Economic growth is strong and so is the job market. This is the kind of environment in which our government should be running surpluses, and yet our deficit could reach $1 trillion next year. What is your plan to reduce our budget deficit?

For Democratic Candidates

Q1: Some in Congress have been citing an idea called modern monetary theory to argue that our national debt isn't really a problem. Do you agree?

Q2: Most Americans agree that the wealthy can and should pay more taxes. But the top 10% of households already contribute 45% of all income tax revenue. Even if we had a federal income tax rate of 50% for upper-income earners, the national debt would still increase. So how can we spend so much on new programs without inevitably requiring more taxes for everyone?

For All Candidates

Q1: Would you support getting rid of the debt ceiling—which has done nothing to control our debt—and replacing it with a Fiscal Responsibility Act, which would force Congress to cut spending or raise taxes once our debt became too large as a share of our economy?

Q2: The whole budget process in Washington is a disaster and it consistently causes destructive government shutdowns. How can we fix the process?

_____

_____

_____

_____

_____

_____

_____

_____

_____

_____

_____

_____

_____

_____

★ 11 ★

GUN SAFETY

On May 7, 2019, two students walked into their school outside of Denver and started shooting, killing one and wounding eight of their classmates. Later that day a *New York Times* report on the tragedy featured the following passage: "'I heard a gunshot,' said Makai Dixon, 8, a second grader who had been training for this moment, with active shooter drills and lockdowns, since he was in kindergarten. 'I'd never heard it before.'"

Read that again: "Since he was in kindergarten."

In America, we now send our five-year-olds to school to learn how to read and count…and to figure out what to do and where to hide if a deranged person enters their class and starts shooting. There is nothing normal or acceptable about living in a society in which any child has to think these thoughts, and it is an indictment of America's broken political system, which has for decades failed to marshal the will to seriously address rampant gun violence and mass shootings.

In the aftermath of each gun massacre, the response from our political class is as predictable as it is infuriating. Thoughts and prayers are offered. Stories of the victims are shared. There are plaintive calls that we must "do something" even as we know little to nothing will be done. The other shootings—the suicides, acts of domestic violence, innocent kids hit by crossfire on a city playground—don't make the national news but are no less horrifying.

THE PROBLEM:
AMERICANS ARE 25 TIMES MORE LIKELY TO BE SHOT AND KILLED WITH A GUN THAN PEOPLE IN OTHER DEVELOPED COUNTRIES

- Almost 40,000 Americans were killed by guns in 2017, the highest level in nearly 40 years. No other developed country comes close.
- Mass and school shootings are a uniquely American phenomenon. As of this writing, there have been 288 school shootings in the United States since 2009 versus 2 in Canada and France, 1 in Germany, and none in Japan, Italy, or the UK.
- In 2018, there were a record high 97 school gun violence incidents in the US—59% higher than the previous record of 59 in 2006.
- The US population is only 5% of the total global population, yet it constitutes 31% of all global mass shooters.

We wrote earlier in the "American Dream" chapter about how easy it is for politicians to cherry-pick data to tell their preferred narrative about the economy. But the data on gun violence in America is overwhelming and irrefutable: As an American, you are much more likely to be killed by a gun than in any other developed country.

The most committed activists on both sides of the gun debate—the Second Amendment defenders and the gun control advocates—recognize this reality and, we believe, share the goal of reducing gun violence. But their proposed solutions seem irreconcilable.

Gun control groups like Everytown for Gun Safety and the Brady Campaign to Prevent Gun Violence propose ideas like restricting access to particular types of guns (assault weapons), expanded background checks, and legal liability for gun manufacturers. Meanwhile, the position of gun rights groups is perhaps best summarized by National Rifle Association (NRA) President Wayne LaPierre, who said in the aftermath of the 2012 massacre of 26 people—including 20 children—at Sandy Hook Elementary School, that: The "only thing that stops a bad guy with a gun is a good guy with a gun."

Decades of public polling data suggest that the American public is closer to the positions of the gun control advocates than that of groups like the NRA. Gallup routinely asks the question, "In general, do you feel that laws covering the sale of firearms should be made more strict, less strict, or kept as they are now?" Their most recent data as of early 2019 found:

+ 61% favor more strict
+ 30% favor kept as they are now
+ 8% favor less strict

As for more specific gun safety policies: A February 2019 Reuters-Ipsos poll found:

+ 82% of Democrats and 63% of Republicans would support raising the legal age to buy a gun from 18 to 21;
+ 90% of Democrats and 73% of Republicans support tracking gun sales through a federal data base;
+ 84% of Democrats and 58% of Republicans support banning high-capacity ammunition clips.

A March 2018 Monmouth poll found 78% of gun owners and 69% of NRA members support required background checks for all gun purchases, which would include gun shows.

But three factors explain why this public sentiment hasn't translated to more robust action to enhance gun safety and reduce violence. First, how Americans view gun issues hinges heavily on how questions are asked and what trade-offs are involved. For example, the Pew Research Center has been asking Americans since the early 1990s whether they think it is more important to "protect the rights of Americans to own guns" or to "control gun ownership." The public has been evenly divided on that question for the last decade. In fact, the percentage of Americans who prioritize protecting gun rights has risen by over ten percentage points since the 1990s. This suggests a reticence among many Americans to embrace gun safety measures that they believe unfairly restrict the rights of law-abiding citizens.

The second factor is the intensity and political engagement of many gun owners. Pew has also surveyed Americans to ask whether they have ever contacted a public official to express their views on gun policy. Twenty-one percent of gun owners reported doing this compared to just 12% of non-gun owners.

And finally, there is this: Many popular gun control measures— like banning assault rifles—may not work. In fact, as we'll explain later, there isn't nearly enough research on which gun safety measures really reduce gun violence.

Amid the charged emotions and lack of dependable information, America has been stuck in an endless cycle of gun violence, followed by outrage and inaction.

It isn't good enough. The challenge for the next president is to start and lead a different kind of conversation on guns—one that respects the rights and views of law-abiding gun owners, that is grounded in facts instead of emotion, and that ultimately leads to reforms that diminish the unconscionable toll that gun violence has on American society.

ANSWERS FROM THE LEFT AND RIGHT

THE LEFT: Ban Assault Rifles

In recent years, many perpetrators of high-profile mass shootings have used the same weapon—an AR-15 assault rifle—to commit their crimes. For entirely understandable reasons, many gun control advocates have fixated on banning these kinds of weapons. But there are a few reasons this approach could be misguided.

For starters, the federal government previously banned assault weapons from 1994 to 2003 with mixed results. The lead author of a comprehensive study on the law's impact concluded, "the ban did not appear to effect gun violence during the time it was in effect. But there is some evidence to suggest it may have modestly reduced shootings had it been in effect for a longer period."

☆ WHY DON'T WE KNOW MORE ☆ ABOUT WHAT CAUSES AND PREVENTS GUN VIOLENCE?

The epidemic of American gun deaths is a public health problem. In the US, the preeminent funder of public health research is the US Centers for Diseases Control and Prevention (CDC). If Americans are dying—be it from car crashes or high cholesterol—CDC-funded research helps figure out why and what to do about it. But in 1996, Rep. Jay Dickey (R-AR) added an amendment to the CDC appropriations bill stating that "none of the funds made available for injury prevention and control at the Centers for Disease Control and Prevention may be used to advocate or promote gun control." Though the Dickey Amendment did not specifically ban research on gun violence, the CDC has for years been hesitant to fund it for fear of political backlash that could jeopardize their other research funding.

Twenty years later, former Rep. Dickey said he had "regrets" about his namesake amendment, lamenting that, "I wish we had started the proper research and kept it going all this time." But the fallout from the Dickey Amendment has been significant.

Although private research is available on the causes of and potential solutions to gun violence, it isn't nearly as comprehensive as research on other public health crises. For example, gun violence received just one twentieth the federal research funds allocated for vehicle accidents between 2004 and 2015, even though they are responsible for a similar number of deaths. As a result, when the nonpartisan Rand Corporation attempted a comprehensive analysis of the costs and benefits of various state gun laws it found, "With a few exceptions, there is a surprisingly limited base of rigorous scientific evidence concerning the effects of many commonly discussed gun policies."

If another assault weapon ban were instituted today, its effectiveness would be further challenged by the ever-changing nature of modern weaponry. As one AR-15 owner explained in a 2016 essay on VOX:

> The AR-15 is less a model of rifle than it is an open-source, modular weapons platform that can be customized for a whole range of applications, from varmint control to taking out 500-pound feral hogs to urban combat. Everything about an individual AR-15 can be changed with aftermarket parts—the caliber of ammunition, recoil, range, weight, length, hold and grip, and on and on.
>
> In the pre-AR-15 era, if you wanted a gun for shooting little groundhogs, a gun for shooting giant feral hogs, and a gun for home defense, you'd buy three different guns in three different calibers and configurations. With the AR platform, a person with absolutely no gunsmithing expertise can buy one gun and a bunch of accessories, and optimize that gun for the application at hand. You can even make an AR-15 into a pistol.

It isn't hard to see how legislation passed today to restrict access to certain kinds of weapons, like the AR-15, would be outrun by innovation tomorrow, especially with the increased use of 3-D printing, which could soon enable many gun owners to print their own weapons and accessories at home.

The AR-15 is a semiautomatic weapon, which means it fires one shot every time the trigger is pulled. Although other countries have been willing to ban semiautomatic weapons—like New Zealand did in the wake of a 2019 mass shooting—almost six in ten Americans told Gallup in 2018 that they would reject such a ban.

For all the attention given to assault rifles, FBI data reveals that they account for only 3% of gun-related homicides in the US. A filing in the Richmond-based Fourth Circuit Court noted "in 2012, the number of AR- and AK-style weapons manufactured and imported into the United States was more than double the number of Ford F-150 trucks sold, the most commonly sold vehicle in the United States," and yet assault rifles were responsible for just 298 homicides in that same year. Handguns, which are also semiautomatic, accounted for over 6,000 homicides.

Other popular gun control measures have delivered similarly mixed results. For example, it is estimated there are currently more guns—almost 400 million—than people in the United States. In an effort to reduce the total supply of guns in circulation, some localities have instituted gun buyback programs. But researchers have concluded gun buybacks often bring in a miniscule number of guns, and most of them are old rifles and revolvers handed in by law-abiding citizens. In other words, gun buybacks don't address the types of people or types of weapons likely to be involved in crimes.

Even expanded background checks are no panacea. As many gun control advocates have noted, 22% of all weapons are purchased without a background check, often through the infamous "gun show loophole."

But as the *New York Times* noted in a 2019 analysis, "A vast majority of guns used in 19 recent mass shootings—including those in Newtown, Conn.; San Bernardino, Calif.; and Las Vegas—were bought legally and after the gunman passed a federal background check."

Of course, just because a given gun safety proposal doesn't work all the time doesn't mean it is not worth pursuing. A single mass shooting prevented by an expanded background check system could arguably make it worth doing. But if we have learned anything over the last two decades of attempted and failed gun safety efforts, it is that getting anything passed into law is hard. So a premium must be placed on ideas that have a good chance of both (1) meaningfully reducing gun violence and (2) passing through the United States Congress.

THE RIGHT: "I Believe in the Second Amendment"

The Second Amendment of the US Constitution articulates the "right of the people to keep and bear arms." There are likely a few people who interpret this language to mean that any person anywhere in America has the right to own any weapon they want—a machine gun, a rocket launcher, grenades—without restriction.

We think this perspective is crazy and thankfully rare. But it does have the virtue of consistency and total adherence to the principle of the Second Amendment.

But once you acknowledge that there can be exceptions to the right to bear arms—that there are instances where it makes sense for the government to restrict who can own a weapon or what they can own—then the blanket "I support the Second Amendment" excuse often used to waive away all gun safety proposals looks pretty lazy.

The debate in America is already settled on whether some gun restrictions are permissible.

They are, so let's stop pretending they aren't. Under longstanding federal law, you can't buy a machine gun. If you are a convicted felon, you aren't allowed—with a few exceptions—to have a gun at all.

For years, the most ardent gun rights activists have been making a version of the "slippery slope" argument in which even the smallest measures to promote gun safety are attacked as the inevitable first step toward a tyrannical future government banning guns and the Second Amendment entirely. It's a nonsense argument, and they should stop making it. The Second Amendment isn't in jeopardy, and it has been reaffirmed repeatedly and recently by the US Supreme Court. But who has earned the right to bear arms—and what arms they can bear—is negotiable, just like everything else in our democracy.

Washington (In)Action on Guns

Since the expiration of the federal assault weapons ban in 2003, Washington has done shockingly little to deal with gun violence. The closest Congress came to significant bipartisan legislation was in the aftermath of the Newtown shooting when Senators Joe Manchin (D-WV) and Pat Toomey (R-PA) proposed an amendment that would have required federal background checks on all commercial sales of guns. It failed by a 54–46 vote in the Senate and was never voted on in the House.

Since that failed vote, Washington has managed to deliver a few constructive reforms even if they fall far short of what is required. In 2018, Congress passed and President Trump signed the Fix NICS

Act, which creates both incentives and penalties to ensure federal agencies report criminal convictions into the national background check system. And in early 2019, the Trump Justice Department banned the "bump stock" that was used by the perpetrator of the 2017 mass shooting in Las Vegas to essentially turn his semiautomatic rifle into a machine gun.

☆ HOW DO FEDERAL GUN ☆ BACKGROUND CHECKS WORK?

According to the Bureau of Alcohol, Tobacco, Firearms, and Explosives, which regulates gun purchases in the US, "licensed firearms importers, manufacturers, and dealers must conduct a NICS [National Instant Criminal Background Check]...prior to the transfer of any firearm to a non-licensed individual." Potential gun purchasers must fill out ATF Form 4473, which requires the purchaser to divulge personal information like their name and address, as well as any criminal history and stays in a mental institution. This information is run through the FBI's database, which in 2017 conducted over 25 million background checks.

But as noted earlier, 22% of all gun purchases occur outside of this federal background check system, at gun shows, online, and in other private party transactions. According to a study cited by the Giffords Law Center to Prevent Gun Violence, 80% of all firearms acquired for criminal purposes are obtained through private-party transfers.

SOLUTIONS:
KEEPING WEAPONS FROM THE WRONG PEOPLE

For the next president to lead a legislative breakthrough on gun violence, they will somehow need to first forge a national consensus on three points.

The first point is that it is about the guns. More specifically—and most importantly—it is about guns in the hands of violent people and criminals. Each time there is an act of mass gun violence, some lawmaker will suggest that the real problem is violent video games. Or lack of mental health treatment. Or poorly secured schools. And these are all fair and relevant points. Restricting kids' access to violent video games and expanding access to mental health would unquestionably help.

But it is about the guns.

You might not know it from the "if it bleeds, it leads" coverage that Americans often see on the news, but violent crime (e.g., rape, murder, assault) in our country is in a multidecade decline. According to the FBI, violent crime fell an astounding 49% between 1993 to 2017. So America is not becoming a more violent nation, relative to our history or to the rest of the world. Some countries in Europe actually have higher rates of violent crime than in the US. But rampant gun violence is a distinctly American phenomenon, and guns in the hands of the wrong people is the prime cause.

The second point upon which the next president must forge agreement is that Washington must act because states and localities can't fix this problem on their own. In 2014, the city of Chicago released a report revealing that 60% of the guns used to commit crimes in the city originated from somewhere else, many from neighboring Indiana and Wisconsin which have much more permissive gun laws. Without a more coherent response from Washington, criminals and people who intend to commit violence will continue to be able to traffic and move weapons across state and city lines with impunity.

If these first two points might require ardent gun rights advocates to give ground, then the third and final point would require a similar compromise from gun control activists. That point is that law-abiding gun owners aren't the problem. A recent study from the University of Pittsburgh found that lawful gun owners are responsible for less than a fifth of all gun crimes, meaning in eight out of ten cases, the perpetrator was someone who illegally possessed a gun. This explains why gun safety measures that are viewed by the public as meting out collective punishment on law-abiding Americans is likely to fail.

Given these realities, here are a few ideas to enhance gun safety that could make a difference and could potentially generate buy-in from both parties.

1. Federal Extreme Risk Protection Orders

In early 2018, *New Yorker* magazine interviewed Josh Horwitz, the executive director of the Coalition to Stop Gun Violence, in which he said:

> A lot of people were saying, if we could just do something about mental health, we could stop something like Sandy Hook. So we looked at the data on that. What we found is that mental illness is not a good predictor of gun violence, but violent behavior is. The biggest risk factor for future violence is past violence. People who break things, get into fights, and threaten people are more likely to be involved in violence in the future. And, if you put a gun in their hands, they are more lethal.

Many states have "extreme risk protection" orders on the books, which permit guns to be temporarily taken from people that family, friends, or law enforcement deem to be a risk to themselves or others. In 2018, Senators Richard Blumenthal (D-CT) and Lindsey Graham (R-SC) proposed legislation that would empower federal courts to issue these extreme risk protection orders. Another bill sponsored by Senators Jack Reed (D-RI), Bill Nelson (D-FL), and Marco Rubio (R-FL) would use incentives to encourage more states to be able to do the same. Each is a good starting point for passing a common sense measure that would keep guns away from violent and dangerous people.

2. Crack Down on Irresponsible Gun Dealers

The ATF reports that 1% of federally licensed firearms dealers are responsible for selling almost 60% of the guns that are found at crime scenes and traced to dealers.

Although the ATF is empowered to shut down gun dealers, the agency has received blowback for targeting small gun stores for innocent paperwork errors. The ATF could benefit from a broader and more flexible range of enforcement tools. In addition to maintaining the right to shut down gun dealers, a bill previously proposed by Sen. Marco Rubio (R-FL) would enable the ATF to levy heavier fines and suspensions.

3. Raise the Gun Buying Age to 21

In early 2019, Republican Senate Majority Leader Mitch McConnell said he'd like to see the age to purchase tobacco raised from 18 to 21. So it is hardly a radical idea for the federal government to put age requirements on the purchase of potentially harmful products. Under current federal law, you must be 21 to purchase a handgun from a licensed gun dealer and 18 to buy "long guns" like rifles and shotguns.

In early 2018, President Trump suggested he would be open to increasing the age requirement for the purchase of certain kinds of weapons.

4. Universal Background Checks

The Manchin-Toomey Universal Background Check bill failed in 2013. And background checks wouldn't solve every act of gun violence.

That doesn't mean expanded background checks aren't still a good idea. A more robust national system—that closes the loopholes allowing purchases online and at gun shows without background checks, but also preserves exceptions for certain legal transfers like those between friends and family—enjoys significant support from the American public.

5. More Gun Violence Research

When Congress passed the Fix NICS Act in 2018, it also included language clarifying the meaning of the Dickey Amendment, stating, "While appropriations language prohibits the CDC and other agencies from using appropriated funding to advocate or promote gun control, the Secretary of Health and Human Services has stated the CDC has the authority to conduct research on the causes of gun violence."

That's a welcome initial step, but making clear a certain kind of research is allowed isn't the same as funding it. That's what is required. The president and Congress should authorize significant new funding into the causes of and solutions to gun violence. This is a public health crisis, and it should be treated accordingly.

6. Look to the States

Amid Washington's inaction, several states, including many with Republican governors and state legislatures, have managed to recently pass reforms with huge bipartisan majorities to keep guns out of the hands of violent people or criminals.

- Nebraska made it a felony for a prohibited juvenile offender to possess a firearm.
- Virginia expanded the scope of a law that prohibited people who had been involuntarily committed to a mental health facility from buying weapons.
- Georgia made it a felony, punishable by up to five years in prison, to "knowingly and intentionally" provide a firearm to a felon.
- Tennessee passed a law requiring law enforcement to be notified when an individual with a history of mental illness attempts to purchase a firearm and fails a background check.
- Louisiana passed legislation giving law enforcement greater authority to seize weapons from domestic abusers.

If states are indeed the "laboratories for democracy," the next president should make a focused effort to determine which measures recently passed at the state level could be scaled nationally.

7. A "Grand Bargain" on Guns

In our research into various proposals to reduce gun violence, we came across several proposals that could make a difference and generate bipartisan support. Many of them are listed above. But even if all these measures were passed, guns would continue to be a singularly contentious issue in American politics. The fighting would inevitably continue. But there was one "grand bargain" idea that was suggested in a *Politico* piece by the guns and technology writer Jon Stokes that we thought broke the mold in the current gun debate and merited further exploration. Here is his proposal:

> The idea is simple but powerful: a federally issued license for simple possession of all semi-automatic firearms. This license would allow us to carefully vet civilian access to semi-automatic weapons, while overriding state-specific weapon bans and eliminating some of the federal paperwork that ties specific firearms to specific owners.
>
> Under a licensing regime that authorizes license holders for possession of semi-autos, it doesn't matter whose semi-auto you're holding, where you got it, how big the magazine is, or how terrifying it looks to the *New York Times* editorial board. It only matters that you've been vetted and are licensed to possess this category of weapon.
>
> The framework I'm proposing is essentially a grand bargain: The gun control side gives up the possibility of a federal gun registry, specific states abandon their weapon bans and long gun registries, and in exchange the gun rights side accepts a brand new federal licensing scheme with real teeth.
>
> If you weren't a license holder, then simple possession of any semi-auto weapon would be a felony. Don't have one on your person, or in your car or home. As for taking possession of the types of guns you could have without a license, then its universal background checks and FFL [Federal Firearms Licensee] (in which the purchaser fills out a paper form that links the gun to the buyer, and second, the seller conducts a federal background check) transfers for you—basically the status quo, in most states.

★2020★
CANDIDATE QUESTIONS

For President Trump

Q1: You have said some Republicans are "petrified" of the NRA. Would you be willing to support a gun safety bill even if the NRA did not support it?

Q2: You have said you support a stronger system of background checks for gun purchases. So does the public. Why haven't you made it more of a priority to work with Congress to get this done?

Q3: Do you still support increasing the age for someone to buy a gun?

For Democratic Candidates

Q1: What's your message to law-abiding gun owners who want to keep guns out of the hands of bad people but also believe strongly in the right of law-abiding citizens to bear arms?

Q2: Do you support an outright ban on the purchase of semiautomatic weapons?

_____

_____

_____

_____

_____

_____

_____

_____

_____

_____

_____

_____

_____

_____

For All Candidates

Q1:   Presidents have been trying, and failing, for decades to pass
laws that can reduce gun violence. Why do you think you can
be any different?

Q2:   Can you identify the one policy that you think would have the
most impact in reducing gun violence in the US?

_____

_____

_____

_____

_____

_____

_____

_____

_____

_____

_____

_____

PART

RESTORING OUR DEMOCRACY

★ 12 ★

FIXING THE SYSTEM

In developing this book, we, along with the research team at The New Center, hoped to uncover meaningful, achievable, and responsible policy solutions to America's toughest challenges. But even as we dug into the minutiae of health care and immigration policy, we were mindful that the biggest barrier to progress in Washington, DC, is not a lack of good policy ideas. There are plenty of great bipartisan white papers floating around. Most of them are gathering dust on shelves somewhere.

The biggest problem is political.

Imagine that you're a member of Congress willing to take on a pressing problem. Addressing it doesn't require you to sacrifice your core political beliefs or principles, but it might require you to agitate parts of your base and some very powerful interest groups. If you act boldly, you might get a few approving nods from editorial boards. But you will also probably get third-party groups running attack ads in your district saying that you betrayed your party and the people you represent. You might get primaried by somebody to your left or right, and if you are already in Congress, the leadership could withhold fundraising support or pull your committee assignments.

We shouldn't be surprised that many leaders choose the easy comfort of the status quo rather than pursuing a bold, but perhaps career-killing, compromise on a big issue. Better to blame the other side and hold on until the next election.

Presidential candidates, who must first navigate a primary election process dominated by left- and right-wing partisans, operate under similar constraints. Our political system—the process through which we elect our leaders and the rules they labor under once they get elected—is broken. That means that even if America is lucky enough to see a perfect storm in which we elect good leaders with good ideas, we can still get bad results.

So here we outline a few big ideas to reform American politics. This certainly isn't an exhaustive list, and there are many others that could merit inclusion. But we believe these three can empower leaders to work together, encourage the cause of national unity, and diminish the power of the extremes that are tearing the nation apart.

☆ **VOTE!** ☆

American politics can be frustrating and infuriating. And all the arguing, fighting, and gridlock makes many people want to just tune out. But the only way to fix our democracy is for more people to tune in and turn out to vote.

In the 2016 election, just 55.7% of voting age Americans voted. This compares to 87% of Belgians, 80% of Australians, 77% of South Koreans, 72% of Israelis, and 63% of Mexicans voting in their recent national elections. Overall, the US places just 26 out of 32 developed nations in citizen voting share.

---

1. National Primary Day

Primary elections, which determine which candidate will represent the Democratic or Republican Party in a general election, are a key driver of the dysfunction in our politics. Because of how primaries work and when they are held, a very small number of Americans decide who leads us.

Races for Congress

Almost 85% of the 435 US House seats are "safe seats," in which candidates from one particular party will almost always win the general election. And this trend keeps getting worse.

In safe seats, the primary election is the only election that really matters in determining who goes to Congress. But primaries are typically low-turnout affairs in which voters are much further to the Right or Left than the general public, which explains how we end up with so many members of Congress on the ideological fringes.

Turnout was actually 50% higher in the 2018 midterms than in the 2014 midterms. That's the good news. The bad news? The 2018 turnout in House primaries was still under 20% of all registered voters.

US HOUSE OF REPRESENTATIVE SEATS 1997-2016

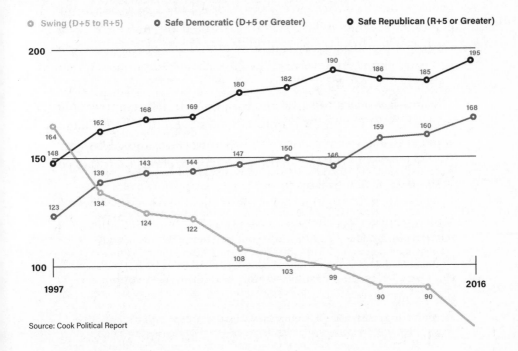

○ Swing (D+5 to R+5)   ● Safe Democratic (D+5 or Greater)   ● Safe Republican (R+5 or Greater)

Source: Cook Political Report

Race for President

In the 2016 presidential election, Americans knew they really had only two choices: Donald Trump or Hillary Clinton.

You might be surprised to learn that those choices were essentially decided for all of us by just 9% of the entire country.

2016 PRESIDENTIAL PRIMARIES: BY THE NUMBERS	
Total Population of US	324,000,000
Total Eligible Voters	231,000,0000
Republican Votes for Donald Trump	14,015,993
Democratic Votes for Hillary Clinton	16,914,722

Turnout is low in primary elections partly because of their unpredictability. Most people know that general elections are on the first Tuesday in November. But unless you are a political junkie, you'd probably have to look up the date and details of your state's primary, which could be held as early as February or as late as the end of the summer in an election year. You'll also find an array of confusing registration rules, different times and places where you can vote, and varying voting dates for the primaries of different state and federal offices.

If you care about the growing, dangerous tribalism in our politics, you need to vote in primary elections. But the government could also make it easier for us all by setting one National Primary Day. States could still decide what kind of elections they want to have (primaries or caucuses).

There are good arguments for why it might make sense to keep a rolling primary calendar for presidential primaries, including the fact that underdog candidates have a better chance to gain traction by spending limited resources in a few early primary states rather than spreading their resources nationally, and we'd support keeping the presidential process largely the same.

But congressional primaries are a different story.

The bottom line is that primary elections are often every bit as important as the general election in deciding who represents us in Congress. So let's make National Primary Day a new tradition.

☆ WHAT ABOUT GERRYMANDERING? ☆

Gerrymandering refers to the practice of politicians drawing state voting district boundaries in a way that can unfairly favor one political party over another. It is sometimes described as politicians picking their voters as opposed to voters picking their politicians. Both parties engage in gerrymandering, and it can be pretty unsavory. But gerrymandering is not the polarization bogeyman that many imagine. It does play a role—and we welcome efforts to combat it—but recent research reveals that a much bigger contributing factor to our political polarization is simple self-sorting.

In other words, Democrats increasingly prefer to live alongside Democrats, and Republicans increasingly prefer to live alongside Republicans.

2. End the Supreme Court Circus

It's hard to imagine now, but Supreme Court justices used to be confirmed in the Senate with huge bipartisan majorities.

+ Anthony Kennedy in 1987:   97–0
+ David Souter in 1990:   90–9
+ Ruth Bader Ginsburg in 1993:   96–3

Senators once believed their constitutional "advise and consent" function meant ensuring that a Supreme Court nominee was professionally qualified and free of any serious ethical concerns. Senators did not expect a nominee to agree with their personal politics, and presidents were given broad latitude to nominate justices who agreed with their judicial philosophy.

Those days are over. Lately, Supreme Court nominations have been consumed by the partisan tribalism that infects almost everything else in our politics.

Look at how the Senate voting has changed for Supreme Court nominees over the last three decades:

VOTES FOR SUPREME COURT JUSTICES

Senate confirmation votes for U.S. Supreme Court Justices since 1986, by party

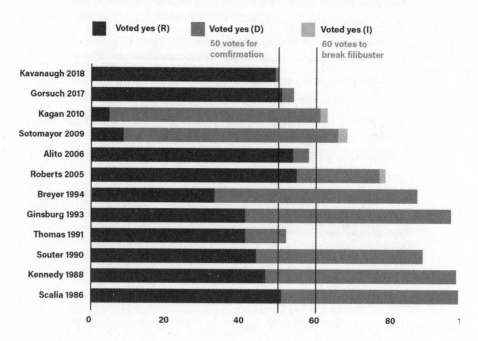

Source: Washington Post, The New York Times

What happened?
Two things:

1. As Congress has become more dysfunctional—and less able to pass legislation to solve our problems and settle tough debates—the court system has become the arbiter of last resort. For partisans on both sides, a Supreme Court nomination is now the ultimate battle for every issue they care about and everything they believe in.

2. Supreme Court justices are serving longer than ever before, with recently retired Justice Anthony Kennedy having served for 30 years.

There is no magic bullet for the first problem of congressional dysfunction. But there is something the next president can do about the second problem.

End Lifetime Appointments to the Supreme Court

Lifetime appointments to the Supreme Court are not explicitly written into the Constitution. But Article III states that justices "shall hold their offices during good behaviour," which has been interpreted to mean that judges can stay on the bench as long as they'd like.

The founders hoped lifetime appointments would shield justices from the political pressures faced by the legislative and executive branches. It was a sensible idea, especially when you consider that most Supreme Court justices didn't initially serve for long. The average retirement age of the first 10 Supreme Court justices was 60 years old, and lifespans were shorter.

But the average American lifespan is now 79 years old, and recent Supreme Court nominees have been getting younger. The last two nominees to the court, Neil Gorsuch and Brett Kavanaugh, are 51 and 54 years old as of 2019. It's not hard to imagine them both sitting on the court in 2050.

- Is this really what the founders intended?
- Why should a president, who serves at most eight years, have the power to shape the Supreme Court and therefore the country for 30 years or more?
- Why should some presidents randomly have the power to nominate three or four Supreme Court judges and others zero or one?

Several polls taken in recent years have shown that two-thirds or more of the public supports an end to lifetime appointments to the Supreme Court. And before he became the Chief Justice of the United States, John Roberts favored term limits, writing that they would "ensure that federal judges would not lose all touch with reality through decades of ivory tower existence [and] also provide a more regular and greater degree of turnover among the judges."

There are several different ideas regarding ways to implement term limits, with one suggesting a new constitutional amendment that would limit Supreme Court justices to a single 18-year term. The terms would be staggered so each president would have a chance to nominate a justice in the first and third years of their own term. And the amendment would need to include instructions to ensure a smooth transition from the current lifetime system to the term-limited one.

Creating term limits for the Supreme Court would require a constitutional amendment—no easy task given that the last one happened over 25 years ago.

But if nothing else, term limits would regularize the Supreme Court nomination and make it less of a no-holds-barred political fight. Eventually, everyone would know and hopefully accept that a president would get to nominate two Supreme Court justices in any four-year presidential term.

3. Universal National Service

Since 1958, Gallup has been surveying Americans' attitudes about marriage, and as you might expect, attitudes have changed significantly over time.

- In 1958, only 4% of Americans approved of interracial marriage. Today, 87% do.
- Twenty years ago, most Americans opposed same-sex marriage. Today, 61% support it.

Prejudice, it appears, is on the decline. Except for one area: Politics.

In 2012, Stanford researchers dug into historical polling data to find that Americans are increasingly likely to say they'd be angry if their child married someone from the opposite political party.

In other words, most Americans are fine with their child bringing home someone from another race or the same gender to Thanksgiving dinner. But the idea of sharing a turkey leg with a Democrat or a Republican? That's unthinkable.

There's no policy that the next president can implement to change hearts and minds. But somehow, people need to see that we are all, first and foremost, Americans. We can be passionate in defending our views. But we can't let ourselves think our neighbor is an enemy just because they think differently.

% UPSET AT MARRIAGE TO MEMBER OF OTHER PARTY

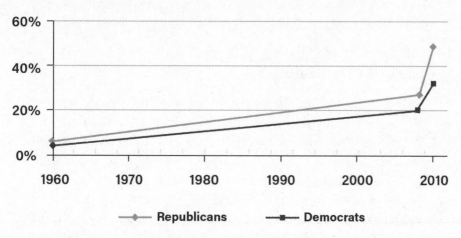

Source: IMF, April 2018

That's how democracies fall apart.

A new program of universal national service is one way for the next president to start healing these divisions and help Americans see how much we have in common with one another. As the journalist Roger Cohen has written, "a vastly expanded, even mandatory, national service program…might at once throw Americans of every creed and culture together for a year or two at an impressionable age, fire up civic engagement and even revive the American dream."

This would require young people to devote one year of their lives to national service, which could take many forms, ranging from military service to rebuilding rural and disadvantaged urban communities to teaching and mentoring. And there's no reason people of other ages—retirees, those out of work—couldn't participate too.

A universal national service program could be built on top of the wildly successful AmeriCorps program, which is overseen by the Corporation for National and Community Service (CNCS). For conservatives uncomfortable with the specter of a big government boondoggle, the private sector could be encouraged to kick in funds through tax credits or incentives, and much of the administration of funding could happen at the state and local level.

Universal national service wouldn't be a panacea. But in bringing together Americans—of different creeds, backgrounds, and political beliefs—to solve problems, it would remind us that what unites us as Americans is so much greater than what divides us.

4. Revive Civic Education

Thomas Jefferson once wrote that "wherever the people are well informed they can be trusted with their own government."

It is hard to argue that Americans are meeting this standard when you consider that a 2016 survey found one in ten college graduates thought Judge Judy was on the Supreme Court. This finding would be pretty funny if it didn't reflect a broad and startling decline in civic awareness across America. Increasingly, Americans don't understand how our government works or the rights and responsibilities of citizenship.

- A 2016 survey by the Annenberg Public Policy Center found that only 26% of Americans can name all three branches of government. A 2015 Annenberg survey found 12% believe the Bill of Rights includes the right to own a pet.
- A 2011 *Newsweek* survey revealed that only 30% believed the Constitution to be the supreme law of the land.
- A 2017 C-Span survey found 57% of Americans could not name a single Supreme Court justice.

This lack of civic knowledge is rooted in a collapse in civic education funding and programs at all levels of the US educational system. According to the American Federation of Teachers, only nine states and the District of Columbia require one year of US government or civics, while 30 states require a half year and the other 11 states have no civics requirement. It's no surprise then that just 24% of 12th grade students scored "proficient" on the 2010 National Assessment of Educational Progress civics test.

As for higher education, a 2016 report from the American Council of Trustees and Alumni surveyed 1,100 liberal arts colleges

and universities and found only 18% required students to take a
course in American history or government. Fixing what's wrong
with American democracy requires citizens who are both more
engaged and informed about how our system works and how change
can happen. Two ideas in particular could start to improve the state
of civic education in the US.

> ◆ *Make Civics a Funding Priority*: Until 2011, the US Depart-
> ment of Education spent a comparatively paltry sum of $35
> million per year on civics education. But then Congress ze-
> roed out the funding entirely. In recent years, Washington
> as well as state governments have understandably ramped
> up their investment in STEM (Science, Technology, Engi-
> neering, and Math) education in an effort to prepare stu-
> dents to get good jobs. But they've neglected to make the
> investment to ensure students become good citizens.
> ◆ *Make High School Graduates Pass the US Citizenship Test*: Sev-
> enteen states require students to pass the US citizenship
> exam before they can graduate high school. The other
> states should follow suit.

5. Regular News Conferences and Question Time for the President

President Dwight Eisenhower once began a news conference by saying: "I will mount the usual weekly cross and let you drive the nails."
He was probably only half-joking. Most presidents don't like news conferences, and it isn't hard to understand why given how adversarial
relations have sometimes been between the president and the press.

That's why recent presidents have given far fewer news conferences than their predecessors.

President Franklin D. Roosevelt averaged nearly six news conferences a month. But over the last two decades, presidents have averaged only about two a month.

In 2017, his first year in office, President Trump had only one solo
news conference.

This isn't good for our democracy. News conferences are a rare opportunity for the media and the American people to break through the spin, speeches, and press releases to force presidents to answer tough questions about pressing issues and to be accountable to the voters who put them in office.

A News Conference Per Month

The next president should commit to holding at least one news conference per month. We want a regular news conference on the agenda—not just when it serves the president's agenda. And to help bring the voice of the voters to the presidency, news conferences should not just be the purview of the traditional press. The president should participate in twice-a-year citizen news conferences where citizens could ask questions via email, Twitter, and other social media platforms. These citizen news conferences should be convened by a media outlet or other neutral third-party organization.

Question Time for the President

The press isn't the only body that deserves more accountability and access from our president. The US should take a cue from the British Parliament's regular questioning of the prime minister to create question time for the president and Congress. These meetings occasionally may be contentious, but at least they force leaders to actually debate one another and defend their ideas.

Here's how it would work: On a rotating basis, the House and Senate would issue monthly invitations to the president to appear in the respective chamber for questions and discussion. Each question period would last 90 minutes and would be televised. The majority and minority would alternate questions. The president could, at their discretion, bring one or more cabinet members to the question period and refer specific questions to them.

6. Regular Bipartisan Meetings

Question time for the president and more regular news conferences would help encourage more transparent debate from our leaders. But these kinds of forums can also turn into forums for showboating and grandstanding for the cameras. In private meetings, leaders can be more up front with one another and actually work together toward compromise.

This is not just a feel-good, symbolic reform. Putting opponents in a room to hash out their differences actually works. It's used in business, diplomacy, and conflict-mediation. In fact, it's one of the few strategies that is proven to make our leaders compromise. In addition to the Camp David Accords, President Reagan's commission on Social Security and the 9/11 Commission all achieved consensus after private meetings, away from the bright lights.

But these meetings are too few and far between. Lately, these private, bipartisan meetings are only held for party leaders and specific committees—and only in worst-case situations when Congress has been unable to come to consensus.

We're living in that worst-case situation every day in Washington.

After the next election, congressional party leaders should form a bipartisan congressional leadership committee as a forum for discussing both legislative agendas and substantive solutions. The committee would meet weekly and (subject to mutual agreement) monthly with the president.

This committee would include the president pro tempore of the Senate, the Speaker of the House, and the Senate and House majority and minority leaders. It would also include four open slots for any two members of the Senate and of the House, which would be determined by lottery on a rotating basis each Congress.

7. Fix (But Don't Dump) the Filibuster

Made famous by the 1939 film *Mr. Smith Goes to Washington* and infamous by senators who used it to block Civil Rights legislation in the 1950s and 1960s, the filibuster was initially conceived as a way to prevent a Senate majority from steamrolling the minority. As long as a senator kept talking on the floor, a bill could not move forward unless a supermajority of senators voted to end the debate. For much of the 20th century, the Senate required a two-thirds majority vote (a device known as cloture) to break a filibuster.

In 1975, the Senate reduced the number of votes required for cloture to three-fifths, or 60 of the current hundred senators.

The filibuster has been used for good and for ill, but for most of the Senate's history, it was rare, and it required members to stand up for hours on end to make their case. Neither is true anymore.

In the first 50 years of the filibuster, it was used only 35 times. Recently, it has been used over 100 times in a single session of Congress.

This practice has frustrated members of both parties, and both President Trump and several Democratic presidential contenders have suggested getting rid of it entirely. But the filibuster—which requires the Senate to get to 60 votes to pass most bills—is one of the few mechanisms remaining that forces members of both parties to try to work together. Were it to be eliminated entirely, we'd likely see even more bills passing with votes from just one party, further increasing the polarization and partisanship in our government.

With that said, there is little question the filibuster is being abused for partisan ends. And each time there is a filibuster, it kicks off a complex set of Senate procedures that effectively brings the institution to a stop for as long as a week and prevents other critical issues from being addressed.

So here's a compromise two-part solution that would preserve the filibuster while significantly decreasing its use:

◆ *Require Real (Not Virtual) Filibusters*: If senators want to halt action on a bill, they must take to the floor and hold it through sustained debate.

◆ *End Filibusters on Motions to Proceed*: Today, filibusters can be used both to prevent a bill from reaching the floor for debate (motion to proceed) and from ultimately being passed. If the Senate simply ended the practice of filibustering motions to proceed, it could cut the number of filibusters in half and allow more issues to be debated and voted on by the full Senate.

8. Bring Back Earmarks

With each passing year, Congress does less and less. Even once-routine actions have become nearly impossible. For instance, in the past 20 years, Congress has failed to pass more than a third of the dozen appropriations bills that it is supposed to complete each year by the end of its fiscal year. Former House Speaker Paul Ryan called the budgeting and appropriations process "irreparably broken."

As for tougher challenges, such as overhauling the nation's deeply troubled immigration system or securing Medicare and Social Security for the long-term, forget it. Effort after effort has gone nowhere, leaving us with a status quo that satisfies almost no one.

Many factors contribute to this gridlock and dysfunction. A key one is that congressional leaders don't have enough tools to persuade rank-and-file members to make concessions and agree to negotiated solutions that can pass the House and Senate. When reluctant lawmakers ask, "What's in it for me and my constituents?" the leaders often lack persuasive answers.

It wasn't always that way. Until 2011, lawmakers could add a limited number of targeted spending items to must-pass bills. These "earmarks" typically directed federal funding for a local bridge, museum, or other project popular with voters back home. These sweeteners made it easier for rank-and-file members to cast tough votes on unpopular but necessary issues, such as raising the debt ceiling.

But some lawmakers and lobbyists abused the earmark system, culminating in the proposed "bridge to nowhere" (a $223 million bridge project that would have connected a small Alaskan city to an island with a population of 50 people). This proved a bridge too far. Amid public outcries, Congress banned earmarks in 2011.

Since then, a number of lawmakers, academics, and advocates have called for restoring earmarks under tight reforms, including divulging the sponsor's name and publishing details for public scrutiny. They note that earmarks don't increase overall federal spending. Instead, they let Congress rather than the executive branch decide where a small portion of funds, already appropriated, should be spent. And they give legislative leaders a tool for building support for difficult bills.

Earmarks are often decried as "pork barrel" spending. But some pork-barreling has been important to American governance since the very start. Consider the Compromise of 1790, essential to the young republic's early progress. Alexander Hamilton prevailed in having the national government assume responsibility for states' debts, and in return, Thomas Jefferson and James Madison of Virginia obtained the national capital (the District of Columbia) for the South.

The ban on earmarks is an unfortunate case of a well-intended good government reform that is very likely making government worse. It is time to give lawmakers reasonable tools to secure support for important bills. Restore the ability to include open allocation of funds to identified projects (a form of earmarks) in appropriations bills, provided the sponsors are publicly identified.

★2020★
CANDIDATE QUESTIONS

For President Trump

Q1: You spoke in your State of the Union speech about how we need to "heal old wounds, build new coalitions, [and] forge new solutions." But you also describe the media as "the enemy of the people." And you say many Democrats in Congress "hate our country." How can you possibly unite the country when you talk this way?

_____

_____

_____

_____

_____

_____

_____

_____

_____

_____

_____

_____

_____

For Democratic Candidates

Q1: There was a poll last year that found that 61% of Democrats thought Republicans were racist, sexist, or bigoted. Do you agree?

_____

_____

_____

_____

_____

_____

_____

_____

_____

_____

_____

_____

_____

_____

_____

_____

_____

For All Candidates

Q1:   As a way to help unite the country, would you support a new
program of universal national service?

Q2:   A Supreme Court justice nominated today could easily sit on
the court for the next 30 years or more. Do you think we should
end lifetime appointments to the Supreme Court?

Q3:   As a way to get Americans to vote in primaries, would you support the creation of a National Primary Day, just like we have
a certain day for the general election?

Q4:   Our political system is so obviously broken. What do you think
is the single most important thing we could do to fix it?

Q5:   Would you commit to regular bipartisan meetings with leaders
of both Houses of Congress throughout your term as president?

Q6:   Would you support Congress bringing back earmarks as a way
to help give members more reasons to support legislation?

THE ROAD AHEAD

The year was 1787 and the US Constitutional Convention that began with so much promise was on the verge of falling apart. At issue was how to share power between the states.

Large states wanted population-based representation in the legislature while smaller states wanted every state to share equal representation. The stalemate wasn't broken until two delegates from Connecticut—Roger Sherman and Oliver Ellsworth—came up with what would appropriately be called the "Connecticut Compromise."

Under the deal, there would be a House of Representatives with delegates assigned according to population and a Senate in which every state would have two members. The divide between the small and large states was bridged, and soon after, a nation was born.

It's a good thing there was no Twitter in 1787 because this compromise would have probably fallen apart once online trolls branded it as the #ShermanSellout.

America's founders are often venerated for their rock-ribbed principles. Less discussed, but no less important, was their belief in the virtue of compromise and their refusal to let the perfect be the enemy of the good. This virtue seems dead in our politics today and on the 2020 campaign trail. But the American people have the ability and the responsibility to demand a restoration of this virtue in the next election. If enough Americans reject division and demand unity from the people competing to win the November 2020 election, these candidates will move in our direction.

In sports, there's a popular phrase used to describe a team that wins even when they don't give a performance they should be proud of. It's called winning ugly. And in sports, it doesn't matter if you win ugly. A win is a win.

But in politics, how you win matters. If you win by barely convincing enough people that you're not as bad as the other side...If you win by just exploiting disappointment and discontent...If you win ugly, in other words, then you won't have a legitimate platform once you're finally elected and positioned to make decisions.

This is essentially where American politics is today and where the 2020 election seems headed.

Demanding that the 2020 candidates offer a vision for how to unite America—as we are here— isn't some pie-in-the-sky, feel-good notion. It's a hard-headed strategy to ensure that our next president has what it takes to govern the country.

Whoever wins in November 2020 won't be a king or a queen. As president, they'll need to push their ideas through a Congress that may be evenly divided and that features a Senate that still requires 60 votes to pass most legislation.

Citizens can't let the 2020 candidates get away with just telling us what they want to do as president. We need a vision for how it gets done, which means a vision for uniting enough of this country and the next Congress behind a workable strategy to solve the problems that matter most to the American people.

NOTES

FOREWORD

viii   it means getting nothing done.: Walsh, M. (2017, October 9). Poll: Americans think Congress should ditch partisanship and embrace compromise. Yahoo News. https://www.yahoo.com/news/poll-americans -think-congress-ditch-partisanship-embrace-compromise-184616902.html

viii   the only election that matters.: Monopoly Politics 2020 (2019). FairVote .org. https://www.fairvote.org/monopoly_politics#overview

viii   than the country at large.: Desilver, D. (2018, October 3). Turnout in this year's U.S. House primaries rose sharply, especially on the Democratic side. Pew Research Center. https://www.pewresearch.org/fact-tank /2018/10/03/turnout-in-this-years-u-s-house-primaries-rose-sharply -especially-on-the-democratic-side/

INTRODUCTION: A NATION DIVIDED

xi   the elites, globalists, and the Left: Montoya-Galvez, C. (2019, March 2). In fiery CPAC speech, Trump blasts Democrats, Mueller probe. CBS News. https://www.cbsnews.com/live-news/trump-speaks-at-2019-cpac-live -updates/

xii   "voice in the national conversation.": The Hidden Tribes of America. (2018). https://hiddentribes.us/#the-exhausted-majority

1. OUR DISRUPTED DEMOCRACY

3   choice in at least 55 years.: McCarthy, J. & Jones, J.M. (2019, February 18). Record high name government as most important problem. Gallup. https://news.gallup.com/poll/246800/record-high-name-government -important-problem.aspx

4   sent a man to the moon.: British Gas. (2017, June 20). Smartphones: More powerful than all of NASA's combined computing in 1969. https:// www.britishgas.co.uk/business/blog/smartphones-more-powerful-than -all-of-nasas-combined-computing-in-1969/.

4   technological change, not trade.: Cocco, F. (2016, December 2). Most U.S. manufacturing jobs lost to technology, not trade. *Financial Times*. https://www.ft.com/content/dec677c0-b7e6-11e6-ba85-95d1533d9a62

4   disrupted by artificial intelligence (AI).: The Associated Press. (2019, January 24). Quarter of U.S. jobs could be jeopardized by AI, research shows. CBS News. https://www.cbsnews.com/news/quarter-us-jobs -could-be-jeopardized-ai-brookings-institution-artifcial-intelligence/

4   solid middle-class income.: Petersen, R. (2016, April 25). The driverless truck is coming, and it's going to automate millions of jobs. *TechCrunch*.

https://techcrunch.com/2016/04/25/the-driverless-truck-is-coming-and
-its-going-to-automate-millions-of-jobs/

4   was tested in Nevada.: Davies, A. (2015, May 5). The world's first self-
driving semi-truck hits the road. *Wired.* https://www.wired.com/2015
/05/worlds-first-self-driving-semi-truck-hits-road/

4   driverless cars on public roads.: Associated Press. (2017, March 8). Uber
self-driving cars are coming back to California roads. FOX Business.
http://www.foxbusiness.com/features/2017/03/08/uber-self-driving-cars
-are-coming-back-to-california-roads.html

5   employment, housing, and health care.: Recognizing the duty of the
Federal Government to create a Green New Deal, H.R. 109, 116th Cong.
(2019).

6   and they have a right to be.: Axelrod, T. (2018, November 27). More than
4 in 5 Americans angry or dissatisfied with Washington: poll. *The Hill.*
https://thehill.com/homenews/news/418456-more-than-4-in-5-americans
-angry-or-dissatisfied-with-washington-poll

6   goals of the Green New Deal.: Kaufman, A.C. (2018, December 17).
Green New Deal has overwhelming bipartisan support, poll finds. At
least, for now. *Huffington Post.* https://www.huffingtonpost.com/entry
/green-new-deal-poll_us_5c169f2ae4b05d7e5d8332a5

2. NO LABELS: BRIDGING THE DIVIDE

11   justice reforms in decades.: Zeller, S. (2019, March 5). Compromise or
resist? Democrats still have a choice to make. CQ Roll Call. http://www
.rollcall.com/news/congress/compromise-resist-democrats-choice

3. THE 2020 UNITY AGENDA

13   "his own opinion, but not his own facts.": Moynihan, D.P. (2010). An
American original. *Vanity Fair.* https://www.vanityfair.com/news/2010
/11/moynihan-letters-201011

17    $1 trillion per year by midcentury.: Kunkle, F. (2015, February 5).
Alzheimer's costs could soar to $1 trillion a year by 2050, report says.
Washington Post. https://www.washingtonpost.com/local/alzheimers
-costs-could-soar-to-1-trillion-a-year-by-2050-report-says/2015/02/04
/441bd16a-ac04-11e4-abe8-e1ef60ca26de_story.html?utm_term=.4a9dd
196a53a

24   "going in the United States.": Gallup. (2019). Satisfaction with the United
States. Gallup. https://news.gallup.com/poll/1669/general-mood-country
.aspx

4. HEALTH CARE

28   of patients in US hospitals.: 10 ridiculously overpriced hospital costs.
(2016, November 21). *MBA Medical.* https://mbamedical.com/blog/10
-ridiculously-overpriced-hospital-charges/

28   costs as much as a Tesla.: Tesla model 3. *Car and Driver.* https://www
.caranddriver.com/tesla/model-3; Understanding knee replacement
costs. What's on the bill? Healthline.com. https://www.healthline.com
/health/total-knee-replacement-surgery/understanding-costs#1

28   life expectancy and infant mortality.: Rapaport, L. (2018, March 13).
U.S. health spending twice other countries' with worse results. Reuters.

https://www.reuters.com/article/us-health-spending/u-s-health
-spending-twice-other-countries-with-worse-results-idUSKCN1GP2YN

28   fast as workers' earnings.: Premiums for employer-sponsored family
health coverage rise 5% to average $19,616; single premiums rise 3% to
$6,616. (2018, October 3). Henry J. Kaiser Family Foundation. https://
www.kff.org/health-costs/press-release/employer-sponsored-family
-coverage-premiums-rise-5-percent-in-2018/

28   compare costs among providers.: Mehrotra, A., Dean, K., Sinaiko, A.,
and Sood, N. (2017, August). Americans support price shopping for
health care, but few actually seek out price information. *Health Affairs.*
https://www.healthaffairs.org/doi/full/10.1377/hlthaff.2016.1471

28   for the same prescription drugs.: Emanuel, E. (2019, March 23). Big
Pharma's Go-To Defense of Soaring Drug Prices Doesn't Add Up. *The
Atlantic.* https://www.theatlantic.com/health/archive/2019/03/drug
-prices-high-cost-research-and-development/585253/

28   paperwork as seeing patients.: Lee, B. (2016, September 7). Doctors
wasting over two-thirds of their time doing paperwork. *Forbes.* https://
www.forbes.com/sites/brucelee/2016/09/07/doctors-wasting-over-two
-thirds-of-their-time-doing-paperwork/#286a77005d7b

28   length of a person's life.: Wang, P. (2012, December 12). Cutting the
High Cost of End-of-Life Care. *Money Magazine.* http://money.com
/money/2793643/cutting-the-high-cost-of-end-of-life-care/

28    $100 billion each year.: Terhune, C., Kaiser Health News (2017, January
8). Leading Republicans see costly malpractice crisis—experts don't.
CNN Business. https://money.cnn.com/2017/01/08/news/economy
/medical-malpractice-republicans/index.html

29   **chart: Where the Health Care Dollars Are Spent:** Kamal, R., Cox, C.
(2018, December 10). How has U.S. spending on healthcare changed over
time? Peterson-Kaiser Health System Tracker. https://www.healthsystem
tracker.org/chart-collection/u-s-spending-healthcare-changed-time/

29   after heart disease and cancer.: Sipherd, R. (2018, February 22). The
third-leading cause of death in US most doctors don't want you to know
about. *CNBC.* https://www.cnbc.com/2018/02/22/medical-errors-third
-leading-cause-of-death-in-america.html

29   were transferred between hospitals.: Usher, M., Sahni, N., Herrigel, D.,
Simon, G., Melton, G.B., Joseph, A., & Olson, A. (2018, May 29).
Diagnostic Discordance, Health Information Exchange, and Inter-
Hospital Transfer Outcomes: a Population Study. *Journal of General
Internal Medicine* 33(9):1447-1453. https://www.ncbi.nlm.nih.gov/pubmed
/29845466

29   information from outside providers.: Holmgren, A., Patel, V., & Adler-
Milstein, J. (2017, October). Progress in interoperability: measuring US
hospitals' engagement in sharing patient data. *Health Affairs.* https://www.
healthaffairs.org/doi/10.1377/hlthaff.2017.0546

30   more than half between 2006 and 2013.: California Maternal Quality
Care Collaborative. Who we are. https://www.cmqcc.org/who-we-are

30   increased by 26.6% from 2000 to 2014.: MacDorman, M., Declercq, E.,
Cabral, H., & Morton, C. (2016, September). Is the United States maternal
mortality rate increasing? Disentangling trends from measurement issues.
Obstetrics & Gynecology 128(3):447–455. https://www.ncbi.nlm.nih.gov
/pmc/articles/PMC5001799/

30   with obstetric services in 2017.: Warshaw, R. (2017, October 31). Health
disparities affect millions in rural U.S. communities. Association of

American Medical Colleges. https://news.aamc.org/patient-care/article/health-disparities-affect-millions-rural-us-commun/

30   the previous five-year period.: Rappleye, E. (2018, October 1). GAO: 10 things to know about the spike in rural hospital closures. *Becker's Hospital Review.* https://www.beckershospitalreview.com/finance/gao-10-things-to-know-about-the-spike-in-rural-hospital-closures.html

30   a tenth of physicians worked there.: Khazan, O. (2014, August 28). Why are there so few doctors in rural America? *The Atlantic.* https://www.theatlantic.com/health/archive/2014/08/why-wont-doctors-move-to-rural-america/379291/

30   in urban areas than rural ones.: National Rural Health Association. About rural health care. https://www.ruralhealthweb.org/about-nrha/about-rural-health-care

30   more in these states than others.: Mason, D. (2017, July 11). Rethinking rural hospitals. *JAMA.* https://jamanetwork.com/journals/jama/full article/2643297; Searing, A. (2018, October 29). More rural hospitals closing in states refusing Medicaid coverage expansion. Georgetown University Health Policy Institute. https://ccf.georgetown.edu/2018/10/29/more-rural-hospitals-closing-in-states-refusing-medicaid-coverage-expansion/

30   killed during the entire Vietnam War.: Soule, D. (2018, November 15). Have more died from opioids in two years than in Vietnam War? PolitiFact. https://www.politifact.com/west-virginia/statements/2018/nov/15/richard-ojeda/have-more-died-opioids-two-years-vietnam-war/

30   specialty treatment in 2016.: Medications to treat opioid use disorder. (2018, June). National Institute on Drug Abuse. https://www.drugabuse.gov/publications/research-reports/medications-to-treat-opioid-addiction/overview

30–   a town with only 2,900 people.: Eyre, E. (2018, January 29). Drug firms
31   shipped 20.8m pain pills to WV town with 2,900 people. *Charleston Gazette-Mail.* https://www.wvgazettemail.com/news/health/drug-firms-shipped-m-pain-pills-to-wv-town-with/article_ef04190c-1763-5a0c-a77a-7da0ff06455b.html

31   first misused prescription opioids.: Prescription opioid use is a risk factor for heroin use. National Institute on Drug Abuse. https://www.drugabuse.gov/publications/research-reports/relationship-between-prescription-drug-heroin-abuse/prescription-opioid-use-risk-factor-heroin-use

31   60 million Americans at or over 65.: CMS Fast Facts (2019). Centers for Medicare & Medicaid Services. https://www.cms.gov/Research-Statistics-Data-and-Systems/Statistics-Trends-and-Reports/CMS-Fast-Facts/index.html

31   the current Medicare program.: Pozen, R. (2019, May 1). 'Medicare for All Isn't Medicare. *Wall Street Journal.* https://www.wsj.com/articles/medicare-for-all-isnt-medicare-11556750380

31   annually over the next 10 years,: Holahan, J., Buettgens, M., Clemans-Cope, L., Favreault, M., Blumberg, L., & Ndwandwe, S. (2016, May 9). The Sanders single-payer health care plan: the effect on national health expenditures and federal and private spending. Urban Institute. https://www.urban.org/research/publication/sanders-single-payer-health-care-plan-effect-national-health-expenditures-and-federal-and-private-spending

31   entire federal budget in 2018.: Amadeo, K. (2019, March 13). FY 2018 Federal Budget: Enacted Versus Trump's Budget Request. The Balance.

https://www.thebalance.com/fy-2018-trump-federal-budget-request
-4158794

32   rise to 79 million by 2030.: Umans, B. & Nonnemaker, K. (2009,
        January). The Medicare beneficiary population. AARP.org. https://
        assets.aarp.org/rgcenter/health/fs149_medicare.pdf

32   pay full benefits by 2026.: Medicare will become insolvent in 2026, U.S.
        government says. (2018, June 5). *LA Times.* https://www.latimes.com
        /nation/nationnow/la-na-pol-medicare-finances-20180605-story.html

32   treatment is becoming more expensive.: Jacobson, L. (2014, September
        9). How much have Medicare beneficiaries 'paid in' to the system?
        PolitiFact. https://www.politifact.com/truth-o-meter/statements/2014
        /sep/09/national-republican-senatorial-committee/how-much-have
        -medicare-beneficiaries-paid-system/

32   health care from their employer,: Kane, A. (2018, October 24).
        Progressives and health care: what comes next? The Progressive Policy
        Institute. https://www.progressivepolicy.org/publications/progressives-
        and-health-care-what-comes-next/; Berchick, E., Hood, E., & Barnett, J.
        (2018, September 12). Health insurance coverage in the United States:
        2017. United States Census Bureau. https://www.census.gov/library
        /publications/2018/demo/p60-264.html

32   receive is "excellent" or "good.": Kane, Progressives and health care:
        what comes next?; Berchick, E., Hood, E., & Barnett, J. (2018, September
        12). Health insurance coverage in the United States: 2017. Reinhart, RJ.
        (2018, February 2). In the news: Americans' satisfaction with their health
        care. Gallup. https://news.gallup.com/poll/226607/news-americans
        -satisfaction-healthcare.aspx

32   repeal, defund, or modify the law.: Riotta, C. (2017, July 29). GOP aims
        to kill Obamacare yet again after failing 70 times. *Newsweek.* https://
        www.newsweek.com/gop-health-care-bill-repeal-and-replace-70-failed
        -attempts-643832

33   the Congressional Budget Office.: Bryan, B. (2017, July 19). The CBO just
        delivered a devastating score for the GOP's Plan B on healthcare. *Business
        Insider.* https://www.businessinsider.com/cbo-score-gop-obamacare-repeal
        -bill-2017-7

33   people with preexisting conditions.: Sullivan, P. (2018, September 12).
        Poll: voters of both parties largely support ObamaCare pre-existing
        condition protections. *The Hill.* https://thehill.com/policy/healthcare
        /406324-poll-large-majorities-of-both-parties-support-obamacare-pre
        -existing

33   when it comes to health care.: Poll: just 13 percent want 'Medicare for
        all' if it means end of private insurance. (2019, February 7). *The Hill.*
        https://thehill.com/hilltv/what-americas-thinking/428958-poll-voters
        -want-the-government-to-provide-healthcare-for

33   up to 122,000 physicians by 2030.: AAMC updates physician shortage
        projections – 122,000 needed by 2032. (2019, April 26). *Healthcare
        Purchasing News.* https://www.hpnonline.com/patient-satisfaction/article
        /21078060/aamc-updates-physician-shortage-projections-122000-needed
        -by-2032

34   health care providers in the US: The New Center (2019, May 1). Closing
        the Doctor Gap. The New Center. http://newcenter.org/the-new-centers
        -closing-the-doctor-gap-solutions-in-brief/

35   "avoid the sick (with narrow networks).": Goodman, J. (2019, March 18).
        Can Democrats And Republicans Strike A Deal On Health Care? *Forbes.*

https://www.forbes.com/sites/johngoodman/2019/03/18/can-democrats
-and-republicans-strike-a-deal-on-health-care/#9799a513919b

36   coverage in many markets.: Koff, S. (2017, August 7). Medicare buy-in for
the age 55-to-64 set: would it make sense? Cleveland.com. https://www
.cleveland.com/nation/index.ssf/2017/08/medicare_buy-in_for_the
_age_55.html

36   "pool of people to cover.": Bodenheimer, T. (2017, October 16). A new
plan to rescue the ACA: Medicare-at-55. *Health Affairs.* https://www
.healthaffairs.org/do/10.1377/hblog20171022.860990/full/

37   would not see it change.: Kane, Progressives and health care: what comes
next?

37   often with better outcomes.: Kamal, R. & Cox, C. (2018, May 8). How do
healthcare prices and use in the U.S. compare to other countries?
Peterson-Kaiser Health System Tracker. https://www.healthsystemtracker
.org/chart-collection/how-do-healthcare-prices-and-use-in-the-u-s
-compare-to-other-countries/#item-on-average-other-wealthy-countries
-spend-half-as-much-per-person-on-healthcare-than-the-u-s

37   each year for these medicines.: Papanicolas, I., Woskie, L., Jha, A., (2018,
March 13). Health Care Spending in the United States and Other High-
Income Countries. *JAMA.* https://jamanetwork.com/journals/jama
/article-abstract/2674671

37   entering clinical trials fail.: Jogalekar, A. (2014, January 6). Why drugs
are expensive: It's the science, stupid. *Scientific American.* http://blogs
.scientificamerican.com/the-curious-wavefunction/2014/01/06/why
-drugs-are-expensive-its-the-science-stupid/

38   new drug is $2.6 billion.: Mullin, R. (2014, November 24). Cost to Develop
New Pharmaceutical Drug Now Exceeds $2.5B. *Scientific American.* https://
www.scientificamerican.com/article/cost-to-develop-new-pharmaceutical
-drug-now-exceeds-2-5b/

38   than any other country in the world.: La Couture, B. (2016, May 18). New
Drug Patents by Country. The American Action Forum. https://www
.americanactionforum.org/weekly-checkup/new-drug-patents-country/

38   even more on sales and marketing.: Lopez, G. (2015, February 11). 9 of 10
top drugmakers spend more on marketing than research. Vox.com. https://
www.vox.com/2015/2/11/8018691/big-pharma-research-advertising

39   of prescription drugs each year.: 10 essential facts about Medicare and
prescription drug spending. (2019, January 29). Henry J. Kaiser Family
Foundation. https://www.kff.org/infographic/10-essential-facts-about
-medicare-and-prescription-drug-spending/

39   from Baptist Health in Miami.: Pear, R. (2019, January 13). Hospitals must
now post prices. But it may take a brain surgeon to decipher them. *New
York Times.* https://www.nytimes.com/2019/01/13/us/politics/hospital
-prices-online.html

39   in the US are "without merit.": Studdert, D., et al. (2006, May 11). Claims,
Errors, and Compensation Payments in Medical Malpractice Litigation.
New England Journal of Medicine 354: 2024-2033. https://www
.nejm.org/doi/full/10.1056/NEJMsa054479

40   potentially caps jury awards.: Lonsdale, J. (2018, October 16). How to
save $900 billion annually in American healthcare. Medium. https://
medium.com/8vc-news/how-to-save-900-billion-annually-in-american
-healthcare-67566b5adb67

40   middlemen" that harms consumers: Edney, A., Langreth, R. (2019,
January 21). Trump Targets Drug Middlemen with 'Devastating' Rebate

Plan. *Bloomberg*. https://www.bloomberg.com/news/articles/2019-01-31
/trump-to-curb-protections-for-drug-rebates-blamed-for-high-costs

40   2% of the population.: Glover, L. (2015, February 6). Why Are Biologic
Drugs So Costly? *U.S. News and World Report*. https://health.usnews.com
/health-news/health-wellness/articles/2015/02/06/why-are-biologic
-drugs-so-costly

41   generic versions of biologics.: Frequently Asked Questions on Patents
and Exclusivity (2018). U.S. Food & Drug Administration. https://www
.fda.gov/drugs/development-approval-process-drugs/frequently-asked
-questions-patents-and-exclusivity

41   currently have an Advanced Directive.: Crist, C. (2017, July 11). Over
one third of U.S. adults have advanced medical directives. Reuters.
https://www.reuters.com/article/us-health-usa-advance-directives/over
-one-third-of-u-s-adults-have-advanced-medical-directives-idUSKBN19
W2NO

41   those who had one ($30,478).: Chambers, C., Diamond, J., Perkel, R.
(1994, March 14). Relationship of Advance Directives to Hospital Charges
in a Medicare Population. *JAMA*. https://jamanetwork.com/journals
/jamainternalmedicine/article-abstract/618526

42   "humankind has ever tried to crack.": Tisch, A. (2018, June 17). Here's
why we should put more money into Alzheimer's research. *The Hill*.
https://thehill.com/opinion/healthcare/392585-heres-why-we-should
-put-more-money-into-alzheimers-research

42   the National Institutes of Health.: Sauer, A. (2018, December 19). U.S.
Congress Approves $425 Million Increase for Alzheimer's Research.
Alzheimers.net. https://www.alzheimers.net/senate-approves-425-million
-increase-for-alzheimers-research/

42   cure for this awful disease.: Tisch, Here's why we should put more money
into Alzheimer's research.

43   "novel insurance plans to flourish.": Lonsdale, How to Save $900 Billion
Annually in American Healthcare.

44   "far less expensive.": Jackson, H. (2017, March 13). 6 promises Trump has
made about health care. *Politico*. https://www.politico.com/story/2017/03
/trump-obamacare-promises-236021; Demoro, R. (2017, March 2). President
Trump's false promises on healthcare. *The Hill*. https://thehill.com/blogs
/pundits-blog/healthcare/322043-president-trumps-false-promises-on
-healthcare

44   less for prescription drugs.: Frakt, A., Pizer, S. & Feldman, R. (2011,
April 14). Should Medicare adopt the Veterans Health Administration
formulary? *Health Economics*. https://papers.ssrn.com/sol3/papers.cfm
?abstract_id=1809665

44   the protections are unconstitutional.: Pear, R. (2018, June 7). Justice
Dept. says crucial provisions of Obamacare are unconstitutional. *New
York Times*. https://www.nytimes.com/2018/06/07/us/politics/trump
-affordable-care-act.html?module=inline

46   53% didn't get enough exercise.: Beck, J. (2016, March 23). Less than 3
percent of Americans live a 'healthy lifestyle.' *The Atlantic*. https://www
.theatlantic.com/health/archive/2016/03/less-than-3-percent-of-americans
-live-a-healthy-lifestyle/475065/

46   what will you do to fix it?: Abelson, R. (2017, September 19). While
premiums soar under Obamacare, costs of employer-based plans are
stable. *New York Times*. https://www.nytimes.com/2017/09/19/health
/health-insurance-premiums-employer.html

48   the third-leading cause of death.: Sipherd, R. (2018, February 22). The third-leading cause of death in US most doctors don't want you to know about. CNBC. https://www.cnbc.com/2018/02/22/medical-errors-third -leading-cause-of-death-in-america.html

48   on opioid addiction treatment.: Lopez, G. (2018, October 24). Trump just signed a bipartisan bill to confront the opioid epidemic. Vox.com. https://www.vox.com/policy-and-politics/2018/9/28/17913938/trump -opioid-epidemic-congress-support-act-bill-law

5. ENERGY AND CLIMATE CHANGE

50   and causing extreme weather.: Monmouth University Polling Institute. (2018, November 29). Climate Concerns Increase; Most Republicans Now Acknowledge Climate Change. https://www.monmouth.edu /polling-institute/reports/monmouthpoll_US_112918/

50   it accounted for 30 years ago.: Fossil fuel energy consumption. (2014). The World Bank Group. https://data.worldbank.org/indicator/EG.USE .COMM.FO.ZS

51   **chart: The World Until 2020**: Thompson, D. (2012, June 20). The economic history of the last 2,000 years: part II. *The Atlantic.* https:// www.theatlantic.com/business/archive/2012/06/the-economic-history -of-the-last-2000-years-part-ii/258762/

52   "weather on ... climate steroids.": Dr. Jane Lubchenco: The 2015 Stephen Schneider Award. (2014, December 16). Climate One.org https://www .climateone.org/events/dr-jane-lubchenco-2014-stephen-schneider-award

52   have occurred since 2001.: Fountain, H., Patel, J., & Popovich, N. (2018, January 18). 2017 was one of the hottest years on record. And that was without El Nino. *New York Times.* https://www.nytimes.com/interactive /2018/01/18/climate/hottest-year-2017.html

52   billion dollars in damage each.: Natural disasters cost U.S. a record $306 billion last year. (2018, January 8). CBS News. https://www.cbsnews.com /news/us-record-306-billion-natural-disasters-last-year-hurricanes-wilidfires/

52   every 100 minutes on average.: The facts on restoring the Louisiana Coast. (2017, November 2). Walton Family Foundation. https://www .waltonfamilyfoundation.org/learning/flash-cards/facts-on-restoring-the -louisiana-coast

53   and influenced by human activity: Scientific consensus: Earth's climate is warming. (2019). NASA.gov. https://climate.nasa.gov/scientific -consensus/

53   their research and methodology.: Foley, K. (2017, September 5). Those 3% of scientific papers that deny climate change? A review found them all flawed. *Quartz.* https://qz.com/1069298/the-3-of-scientific-papers -that-deny-climate-change-are-all-flawed/

53   "the rate of economic growth.": Fourth National Climate Assessment. (2017). U.S. Global Change Research Program. https://nca2018.global change.gov/

53   "and other forms of violence.": Quadrennial Defense Review 2014. (2014). U.S. Department of Defense. http://archive.defense.gov/pubs /2014_Quadrennial_Defense_Review.pdf

54   **table: Low-end Levelized Cost ($/MWh) of Electricity by Source 2018**: Levelized cost of energy and levelized cost of storage 2018. (2018, November 8). Lazard. https://www.lazard.com/perspective/levelized -cost-of-energy-and-levelized-cost-of-storage-2018/

54 activities like manufacturing, transportation, etc.: Morris, D. (2018, February 18). Renewable energy surges to 18% of U.S. power mix. *Fortune.* http://fortune.com/2018/02/18/renewable-energy-us-power -mix/; Frequently Asked Questions. (2018, May 18). U.S. Energy Information Administration. https://www.eia.gov/tools/faqs/faq.php ?id=92&t=4

54 technologies currently available today.: Renewable Electricity Futures Study. (2012). National Renewable Energy Laboratory, U.S. Department of Energy. https://www.nrel.gov/analysis/re-futures.html

55 **chart: It's All About the Batteries**: Randall, T. (2016, February 25). Here's How Electric Cars Will Cause the Next Oil Crisis. *Bloomberg.* https://www.bloomberg.com/features/2016-ev-oil-crisis/

55 is falling by 20% per year.: Frankel, D., Kane, S., & Tryggestad, C. (2018, June). The new rules of competition in energy storage. McKinsey & Company. https://www.mckinsey.com/industries/electric-power-and -natural-gas/our-insights/the-new-rules-of-competition-in-energy-storage

55 decreased by 2.7% between 2016 and 2017.: Data shows decrease in U.S. greenhouse gas emissions during Trump's first year in office. (2018, October 17). Environmental Protection Agency. https://www.epa.gov /newsreleases/data-shows-decrease-us-greenhouse-gas-emissions-during -trumps-first-year-office

55 as the average person in China.: Pettinger, T. (2017, October 25). Top CO2 polluters and highest per capita. Economicshelp.org. https://www .economicshelp.org/blog/10296/economics/top-co2-polluters-highest -per-capita/

56 the answer is not much: Bryce, R. (2010, May 11). The real problem with renewables. *Forbes.* https://www.forbes.com/2010/05/11/renewables -energy-oil-economy-opinions-contributors-robert-bryce.html#6544ea 7c1403

56 twice the size of California.: Bryce, R. (2018, October 30). Why wind power isn't the answer. *City Journal.* https://www.city-journal.org/wind -power-is-not-the-answer

57 Atmosphere for Between 20-200 Years: Clark, D., Carbon Brief (2012, January 16). How long do greenhouse gases stay in the air? *The Guardian.* https://www.theguardian.com/environment/2012/jan/16/greenhouse -gases-remain-air

57 from fossil fuels were halted.: Kehse, U., Max Planck Society (2017, October 3). Global warming doesn't stop when the emissions stop. Phys .org. https://phys.org/news/2017-10-global-doesnt-emissions.html

58 of all global carbon emissions.: Graham, K. (2018, May 14). Company debuts world's first fossil-free steel-making technology. *Digital Journal.* http://www.digitaljournal.com/tech-and-science/technology/new-pilot -facility-in-sweden-to-produce-steel-without-fossil-fuel/article/522179

58 accounting for most of the rest.: How is steel produced? (2017). World Coal Association. https://www.worldcoal.org/coal/uses-coal/how-steel -produced

58 transportation and electricity generation.: Meyer, R. (2019, February 19). A centuries-old idea could revolutionize climate policy. *The Atlantic.* https://www.theatlantic.com/science/archive/2019/02/green-new-deal -economic-principles/582943/

58 "gas and coal will fill the void.": The Nuclear Power Dilemma. (2018). Union of Concerned Scientists. https://www.ucsusa.org/nuclear-power /cost-nuclear-power/retirements

58   of all coal plants in the US.: Nguyen Ly, M. (2018, October 7). China building coal plants equal to entire US capacity. *The Epoch Times.* https://www.theepochtimes.com/china-building-new-coal-plants-equal-to-entire-us-capacity_2679901.html

58   of all global energy use.: Renewables can't save the planet. Only nuclear can. (2017, August 16). Environmental Progress. http://environmental progress.org/big-news/2017/8/16/renewables-cant-save-the-planet-only-nuclear-can

59   **chart: 2014 Global CO₂ Emissions from Fossil Fuel Combustion and Some Industrial Processes**: Global greenhouse gas emissions data. (2014). Environmental Protection Agency. https://www.epa.gov/ghgemissions/global-greenhouse-gas-emissions-data

59   Not Have Access to Electricity: 5 Facts You Should Know About Energy Poverty. (2017, April 17). FINCA International. https://finca.org/blogs/5-facts-you-should-know-about-energy-poverty/

60   "transportation and other infrastructure.": Select committee for a Green New Deal draft text. (2019). Scribd. https://www.scribd.com/document/394390447/Select-Committee-for-a-Green-New-Deal-Draft-Text; Britschgi, C. (2019, February 8). Zoning makes the Green New Deal impossible. Reason. https://reason.com/2019/02/08/zoning-makes-the-green-new-deal-impossib

60   "Global warming is an expensive hoax!": Schulman, J. (2018, December 12). Every insane thing Donald Trump has said about global warming. *Mother Jones.* https://www.motherjones.com/environment/2016/12/trump-climate-timeline/

60   system to reduce carbon emissions.: Revkin, A., Carter, S., Ellis, J., Hossain, F., & Mclean, A. (2008). On the issues: climate change. *New York Times.* https://www.nytimes.com/elections/2008/president/issues/climate.html

61   almost 840,000 Americans into poverty.: Plenty at stake: indicators of American energy insecurity. (2014, September). U.S. Senate Committee on Energy & Natural Resources. https://www.energy.senate.gov/public/index.cfm/files/serve?File_id=075f393e-3789-4ffe-ab76-025976ef4954

61   prices and economic upheaval.: The End of Oil: On the Edge of a Perilous New World. (2004, May 15). Amazon.com. https://www.amazon.com/End-Oil-Edge-Perilous-World/dp/0618239774

61   barrels of proven oil reserves.: United States Country Analysis Brief. (2003, May). U.S. Energy Information Association. https://www.geni.org/globalenergy/library/national_energy_grid/united-states-of-america/UnitedStatesCountryAnalysis.shtml

61   more than Saudi Arabia or Russia.: Nysveen, P.M. (2016, July). U.S. holds most recoverable oil reserves. *The American Oil & Gas Reporter.* https://www.aogr.com/web-exclusives/exclusive-story/u.s.-holds-most-recoverable-oil-reserves

62   "You cannot diminish DOE's involvement.": U.S. Government Role in Shale Gas Fracking History: A Response to Our Critics (2012, March). The Breakthrough Institute. https://thebreakthrough.org/issues/energy/us-government-role-in-shale-gas-fracking-history-a-response-to-our-critics

63   and health has consumed 20–25%.: Federal investment in research and development spurs U.S. competitiveness. (2015, February). The Pew Charitable Trusts. https://www.pewtrusts.org/~/media/assets/2015/02/cleanenergy_combined_fact_sheets.pdf?la=en

64 Macron announced a new fuel tax.: Borenstein, S. & Charleton, A. (2018, December 6). Paris riots over fuel taxes dim hopes for climate fight. *AP News.* https://www.apnews.com/8b9d12d3605b4f6fa989c5377393d547

65 to prop up the failing coal industry?: Heikkinen, N. (2018, September 17). 8 ways that EPA's helping the coal industry. *E&E News.* https://www.eenews.net/stories/1060097285

6. INFRASTRUCTURE

71 But the overall grade? D+.: 2017 infrastructure report card. (2019). American Society of Civil Engineers. https://www.infrastructurereportcard.org/americas-grades/

72 car repairs and wasted fuel.: Read, R. (2017, April 27). America, we have an infrastructure problem, and this documentary is here to explain it. *Washington Post.* https://www.washingtonpost.com/cars/america-we-have-an-infrastructure-problem-and-this-documentary-is-here-to-explain-it/2017/04/27/a32cedd8-2b7d-11e7-9081-f5405f56d3e4_story.html?utm_term=.b27d02a284ed

72 42 hours delayed in traffic.: Walpole, B. (2017, March 30). 5 ways underfunding infrastructure affects you. American Society of Civil Engineers. https://news.asce.org/5-ways-underfunding-infrastructure-affects-you/

72 11,000 Olympic swimming pools.: Sherraden, S. and Henry, S. (2011, March 2). Costs of the infrastructure deficit. New America. https://www.newamerica.org/economic-growth/policy-papers/costs-of-the-infrastructure-deficit/

72 fill over 11 million bathtubs.: Navales, E. (2016, July). Paying the price. International Right of Way Association. http://eweb.irwaonline.org/eweb/upload/web_jul_aug_16_PayingthePrice.pdf

72 Environmental Protection Agency's allowable limit.: Ingraham, C. (2017, September 21.) Flint's lead-poisoned water had a 'horrifyingly large' effect on fetal deaths, study finds. *Washington Post.* https://www.washingtonpost.com/news/wonk/wp/2017/09/21/flints-lead-poisoned-water-had-a-horrifyingly-large-effect-on-fetal-deaths-study-finds/?utm_term=.a286ca87f9cb

72 poisoning among children than Flint.: Ross, J. (2016, February 12). Here are the stunning social costs of the Flint water crisis. *Washington Post.* https://www.washingtonpost.com/news/the-fix/wp/2016/02/12/here-are-the-stunning-social-costs-of-the-flint-water-crisis/?utm_term=.d65bbf89a458

73 don't have access to it either.: Blackwell, A. G. (2017, June 9). Infrastructure is not just roads and bridges. *New York Times.* https://www.nytimes.com/2017/06/09/opinion/infrastructure-public-transportation-broadband.html?_r=0); Enderle, J. (2018, April 1). More on high-speed access (or lack of it) in U.S. schools. School Planning & Management. https://webspm.com/articles/2018/04/01/high-speed-access.aspx

73 graduation rates than those who don't.: Dilley, J. (2018, August 28). States with access to faster internet have more successful people. HighSpeedInternet.com. https://www.highspeedinternet.com/resources/states-with-access-to-faster-internet-have-more-successful-people/

73 1.5 million jobs to the economy.: Woetzel, J., Garemo, N., Mischke, J., Hjerpe, M., & Palter, R. (2016, June). Bridging global infrastructure gaps. McKinsey & Company. https://www.mckinsey.com/industries

/capital-projects-and-infrastructure/our-insights/bridging-global
-infrastructure-gaps

73   will cost some 2.5 million jobs.: McCarthy, N. (2017, March 13). The massive cost of America's crumbling infrastructure. *Forbes.* https://www .forbes.com/sites/niallmccarthy/2017/03/13/the-massive-cost-of-americas -crumbling-infrastructure-infographic/#2acde3c73978

73   infrastructure up to a B grade.: Economic impact. (2016). American Society of Civil Engineers. https://www.infrastructurereportcard.org/the -impact/economic-impact/

73   as much as the US on infrastructure.: Woetzel, J., Garemo, N., Mischke, J., Hjerpe, M., & Palter, R., Bridging global infrastructure gaps.

74   "costly and, often, environmentally destructive.": Accelerate infrastructure permitting. (2017, March). Common Good. https://www .commongood.org/wp-content/uploads/2017/10/Infrastructure -Permitting-Language-March-20171.pdf

74   US and global infrastructure.: Financial Times (2019, January 19). Infrastructure funds set for boom year after record 2018. *Financial Times.* https://www.ft.com/content/933a657f-6421-30a5-bbd2-14c107a44700

74–   signed into law months earlier.: Senate Democrats. (2018, March 7).
75   Senate Democrats' jobs & infrastructure plan for America's workers. https://www.democrats.senate.gov/imo/media/doc/Senate%20 Democrats'%20Jobs%20and%20Infrastructure%20Plan.pdf

75   private sector infrastructure investments.: Trump, D. J. (2018, February 12). Building a stronger America: President Donald J. Trump's American infrastructure initiative. WhiteHouse.gov. https://www.whitehouse.gov /briefings-statements/building-stronger-america-president-donald-j -trumps-american-infrastructure-initiative/

75   "infrastructure is done by the public sector.": Shirley, C. (2017, March 1). Spending on infrastructure and investment. Congressional Budget Office. https://www.cbo.gov/publication/52463

75   built in the past half-century.: ASCE, Economic impact.

75   take a decade or more in the US: Smith, N. (2017, May 31). The U.S. has forgotten how to do infrastructure. *Bloomberg.* https://www.bloomberg .com/view/articles/2017-05-31/the-u-s-has-forgotten-how-to-do -infrastructure

76   interstate highway repair and operation.: Poole, R. (2019, April 8). If You Drive, You Should Pay. *Wall Street Journal.* https://www.wsj.com/articles /if-you-drive-you-should-pay-11554761187

77   double the cost of large projects.: Howard, P. K. (2017, April 2). Shred the red tape: To fix America's infrastructure, Congress must attack laws - and grow courage on taxes. *New York Daily News.* http://www.nydaily news.com/opinion/shred-red-tape-build-infrastructure-article-1.3015542

77   determine what communities actually need.: Daniels, J. (2018, March 12). California's $77 billion 'bullet train to nowhere' faces a murky future as political opposition ramps up. CNBC. https://www.cnbc.com /2018/03/12/californias-77-billion-high-speed-rail-project-is-in-trouble .html

81   "there is no such thing as shovel-ready projects.": Baker, P. (2010, October 12). Education of a president. *New York Times.* https://www.nytimes.com /2010/10/17/magazine/17obama-t.html?_r=3&ref=magazine&pagewanted =all%22

7. THE RISE OF BIG TECH

85   "to the creepy line and not cross it.": Saint, N. (2010, October 1). Eric
        Schmidt: Google's policy is to "get right up to the creepy line and not
        cross it." *Business Insider*. https://www.businessinsider.com/eric-schmidt
        -googles-policy-is-to-get-right-up-to-the-creepy-line-and-not-cross-it
        -2010-10

85   new customers under false pretenses.: Roberts, J. J. (2015, September 3).
        Apple, Google, Intel, Adobe will pay $415 million in anti-poach deal.
        Fortune. http://fortune.com/2015/09/03/koh-anti-poach-order/; Scott,
        M. (2017, June 27). Google fined record $2.7 billion in E.U. antitrust
        ruling. *New York Times*. https://www.nytimes.com/2017/06/27/
        technology/eu-google-fine.html; Scott, M. (2016, March 2). Facebook
        faces German antitrust investigation. *New York Times*. https://www
        .nytimes.com/2016/03/03/business/international/facebook-faces-german
        -antitrust-investigation.html?_r=0.

85   the personal data of their users.: The New Center's Big Tech Solutions in
        Brief. (2018, November 26). The New Center. http://newcenter.org/the
        -new-center-big-tech-solutions-in-brief/

86   businesses from doing the same thing.: Hathaway, I. and Litan, R.E.
        (2014, November 20). What's driving the decline in the firm formation
        rate? A partial explanation. The Brookings Institution. https://www
        .brookings.edu/research/whats-driving-the-decline-in-the-firm-formation
        -rate-a-partial-explanation/

86   the World's Most Admired Companies.: Fortune (2017). The world's most
        admired companies for 2017. http://fortune.com/worlds-most-admired
        -companies/list/.

86   third of the fund's recent gains.: Imbert, F. (2017, May 30). Amazon and
        other tech giants account for a third of stock gains; Now that could be a
        problem. CNBC. https://www.cnbc.com/2017/05/30/big-tech-accounts
        -for-a-third-of-stock-gains-but-that-could-hurt-the-market.html.

86   split into the "Baby Bells" in 1984.: Thompson, D. (2016, September 11).
        America's monopoly problem. *The Atlantic*. https://www.theatlantic.com
        /magazine/archive/2016/10/americas-monopoly-problem/497549/;
        Pagliery, J. (2014, May 20). How AT&T got busted up and pieced back
        together. CNN Business. http://money.cnn.com/2014/05/20/technology
        /att-merger-history/index.html.

87   that explicitly requires location.: The New Center. (2018, November 26).
        Big Tech: Public Discourse and Privacy. https://cloudfront.newcenter.org
        /wp-content/uploads/2018/11/26062745/Big-Tech-Policy-Paper2.pdf

87   services in your Google account.: The Associated Press. (2018, August 13).
        Google records your location even when you tell it not to. *The Guardian*.
        https://www.theguardian.com/technology/2018/aug/13/google-location
        -tracking-android-iphone-mobile

87   third-party tracking companies.: Vallina-Rodriguez, N. and Sudaresan,
        S. (2017, May 29). 7 in 10 smartphone apps share your data with third
        party services. The Conversation. http://theconversation.com/7-in-10
        -smartphone-apps-share-your-data-with-third-party-services-72404

87   bail bondsmen and bounty hunters.: Cox, J. (2019, January 8). I gave a
        bounty hunter $300. Then he located our phone. *Vice*. https://mother
        board.vice.com/en_us/article/nepxbz/i-gave-a-bounty-hunter-300-dollars
        -located-phone-microbilt-zumigo-tmobile

87   Facebook messages without explicit consent.: Dance, G., LaForgia, M.,
        and Confessore, N. (2018, December 18). As Facebook raised a privacy

wall, it carved an opening for tech giants. *New York Times.* https://www
.nytimes.com/2018/12/18/technology/facebook-privacy.html

88   eight additional clicks to return to Facebook.: Big Tech: Public Discourse
and Privacy. (2018, November 25). The New Center. http://newcenter.org
/big-tech-public-discourse-and-privacy/

88   or a company owned by Facebook.: Ip, G. (2018, January 16). The
Antitrust Case against Facebook, Google, and Amazon. *Wall Street Journal.*
https://www.wsj.com/articles/the-antitrust-case-against-facebook-google
-amazon-and-apple-1516121561

89   internet search is controlled by Google.: StatCounter. (2019). Search
engine market share worldwide. http://gs.statcounter.com/search
-engine-market-share

89   are made by Apple or Google.: Statista. (2018). Subscriber share held by
smartphone operating systems in the United States from 2012 to 2018.
https://www.statista.com/statistics/266572/market-share-held-by-smart
phone-platforms-in-the-united-states/

89   crude oil market share at its peak.: Ip, The Antitrust Case Against
Facebook, Google, and Amazon.

89   spent online goes through Amazon.: Lunden, I. (2018, July 13).
Amazon's share of the US e-commerce market is now 49%, or 5% of all
retail spend. *TechCrunch.* https://techcrunch.com/2018/07/13/amazons
-share-of-the-us-e-commerce-market-is-now-49-or-5-of-all-retail-spend/

89   are made by Facebook or Google.: Hartmans, A. (2017, August 29).
These are the 10 most used smartphone apps. *Business Insider.* https://
www.businessinsider.com/most-used-smartphone-apps-2017-8

91   company made money by selling advertisements.: Sullivan, M. (2018,
April 10). Members of Congress can't possibly regulate Facebook. They
don't understand it. *Washington Post.* https://www.washingtonpost.com
/lifestyle/style/members-of-congress-cant-possibly-regulate-facebook
-they-dont-understand-it/2018/04/10/27fa163e-3cd1-11e8-8d53-eba0
ed2371cc_story.html?utm_term=.3c40e219d66d

92   similar to those that now exist in Europe.: Shaban, H., Romm, T. (2019,
January 30). Apple escalates war against Facebook and its privacy
practices. *Washington Post.* https://www.washingtonpost.com/technology
/2019/01/30/facebook-paid-teens-use-research-app-that-could-monitor
-online-activity-communication/?utm_term=.f57f0114c908

94   the internet browser software market.: Keaten, J., and Moore, J. F. (1998,
May 18). U.S., states sue Microsoft for antitrust. CNN Business. http://
money.cnn.com/1998/05/18/technology/microsoft_suit/

95   "so biased towards the Dems it is ridiculous!": Lomas, N. (2018,
December 18). Facebook's got 99 problems but Trump's latest 'bias'
tweet ain't one. *TechCrunch.* https://techcrunch.com/2018/12/18
/facebooks-got-99-problems-but-trumps-latest-bias-tweet-aint-one/

97   received so many contributions from it?: Bowden, J. (2018, October 26).
Tech workers' political donations overwhelmingly skew Democratic:
report. *The Hill.* https://thehill.com/policy/technology/413428-tech
-workers-political-donations-skew-overwhelmingly-democratic-report

8. THE AMERICAN DREAM

101   "each according to ability or achievement.": Library of Congress. What
is the American Dream? Retrieved from http://www.loc.gov/teachers
/classroommaterials/lessons/american-dream/students/thedream.html

101   published called *How to Lie with Statistics.*: Huff, D. (1993). *How to Lie with Statistics.* https://www.amazon.com/How-Lie-Statistics-Darrell-Huff/dp /0393310728

101   "economy in the HISTORY of America.": Long, H. (2018, June 5). Trump says U.S. economy may be the 'greatest in history.' Let's check the record. *Washington Post.* https://www.washingtonpost.com/news/wonk/wp/2018 /06/05/trump-says-u-s-economy-may-be-the-greatest-in-history-lets-check -the-record/?utm_term=.19671e7e8015

101   the lowest in almost 50 years.: Ibid.

101   "of wealth and income inequality.": Dews, F. (2015, February 9). Sen. Bernie Sanders: We have a government of, by, and for billionaires. The Brookings Institution. https://www.brookings.edu/blog/brookings-now/2015/02/09 /sen-bernie-sanders-we-have-a-government-of-by-and-for-billionaires/

101   at any point since the 1920s.: Covert, B. (2014, March 31). Wealth inequality is now as bad as it was during the 1920s. ThinkProgress. https:// thinkprogress.org/wealth-inequality-is-now-as-bad-as-it-was-during-the -1920s-7ec5cebcfc3/

102   government food and housing assistance.: Burtless, G. (2014, May 20). Has rising inequality brought us back to the 1920s? It depends on how we measure income. The Brookings Institution. https://www.brookings .edu/blog/up-front/2014/05/20/has-rising-inequality-brought-us-back -to-the-1920s-it-depends-on-how-we-measure-income/

102   compared to 37% in 1979.: Pethokoukis, J. (2016, June 21). The US middle class is disappearing... into the upper middle class. But there's more to the story... American Enterprise Institute. http://www.aei.org /publication/the-us-middle-class-is-disappearing-into-the-upper-middle -class-but-theres-more-to-the-story/

102   the lower-middle class or poverty.: Ibid.

102   43% saying it's on the wrong track.: Harvard-Harris. (2019). Monthly Harvard-Harris Poll: January 2019. https://harvardharrispoll.com/wp -content/uploads/2019/01/Jan2019_HHP_registeredvoters_topline.pdf

103   a 49-year low of 3.7% in late 2018.: Ferreira, J. (2019, February 1). United States unemployment rate. Trading Economics. https://tradingeconomics .com/united-states/unemployment-rate

103   a city that has a population over 50,000.: Swenson, D. (2019, May 12). Opinion: Dwindling population and disappearing jobs is the fate that awaits much of rural America. *MarketWatch.* https://www.marketwatch .com/story/much-of-rural-america-is-fated-to-just-keep-dwindling-2019 -05-07?mod=mw_theo_homepage

103   their fastest rate in a decade.: Long, H. (2019, March 8). Workers suddenly have more power to demand higher pay and better jobs. *Washington Post.* https://www.washingtonpost.com/business/economy /workers-suddenly-have-more-power-to-demand-higher-pay-and-better -jobs/2019/03/08/6668659c-41bc-11e9-9361-301ffb5bd5e6_story.html ?utm_term=.f547c5b68c7b

103   purchasing power as it did 40 years ago.: Desilver, D. (2018, August 7). For most U.S. workers, real wages have barely budged in decades. Pew Research Center. http://www.pewresearch.org/fact-tank/2018/08/07 /for-most-us-workers-real-wages-have-barely-budged-for-decades/

103   available workers to fill them.: Cox, J. (2018, June 5). There are more jobs than people out of work, something the American economy has never experienced before. CNBC. https://www.cnbc.com/2018/06/05 /there-are-more-jobs-than-people-out-of-work.html

103   a job has dropped by half.: White, M. (2017, May 9). There's no place like home: Fewer Americans are moving for work. NBC News. https://www .nbcnews.com/business/consumer/there-s-no-place-home-fewer-americans -are-moving-work-n756741

103   workforce reached an all-time high.: Jones, S. (2018, April 6). 72,548,000: Record number of women employed in March. CNSNews.com. https:// www.cnsnews.com/news/article/susan-jones/72548000-record-number -women-employed-march

103   there are three who are not looking at all.: Mankiw, G. (2018, June 15). Why aren't more men working? *New York Times*. https://www.nytimes .com/2018/06/15/business/men-unemployment-jobs.html

103   funding was invested in 2018.: Rowley, J. (2019, January 7). Q4 2018 closes out a record year for the global VC market. CrunchBase. https:// news.crunchbase.com/news/q4-2018-closes-out-a-record-year-for-the -global-vc-market/

103   Boston, New York City, and Washington, DC.: Florida, R. (2018, March 27). The extreme geographic inequality of high-tech venture capital. CityLab. https://www.citylab.com/life/2018/03/the-extreme-geographic -inequality-of-high-tech-venture-capital/552026/

103   bachelor's degree—the most ever.: Wilson, R. (2017, April 3). Census: More Americans have college degrees than ever before. *The Hill*. https:// thehill.com/homenews/state-watch/326995-census-more-americans -have-college-degrees-than-ever-before

103    $37,712 for every student borrower.: Friedman, Z. (2018, June 13). Student loan debt statistics in 2018: A $1.5 trillion crisis. *Forbes*. https:// www.forbes.com/sites/zackfriedman/2018/06/13/student-loan-debt -statistics-2018/#1a4cc507310f

103    $500 billion on higher education.: Sharp, K. and Kinder, M. (2018, April 21). The problem with the American workforce. *The Week*. https://theweek .com/articles/767951/problem-american-workforce

103    $8 billion on worker training.: Ibid.

103   market hit a record high in 2018.: Chang, S. and Vlastelica, R. (2018, October 2). Dow closes at record for the 14th time in 2018 even as trade fears simmer. *MarketWatch*. https://www.marketwatch.com/story/stock -futures-fall-trade-and-italy-remain-in-focus-2018-10-02

103   54% of US families own stocks.: Wile, R. (2017, December 19). The richest 10% of Americans now own 84% of all stocks. *Money Magazine*. http://money.com/money/5054009/stock-ownership-10-percent-richest/

103   new record high of $106,500 in 2018.: Shell, A. (2018, November 5). 401(K) account balance hits record high of $106,500; where do you stack up? *USA Today*. https://www.usatoday.com/story/money/2018/11/05/401 -k-account-balance-hits-record/1890029002/

103   one in four non-retired adults has no retirement savings or pension.: Board of Governors of the Federal Reserve System. (2018, June 19). Report on the Economic Well-Being of U.S. Households in 2017 - May 2018. https://www.federalreserve.gov/publications/2018-economic-well -being-of-us-households-in-2017-executive-summary.htm

103   doubled since the depths of the Great Recession.: Board of Governors of the Federal Reserve System. (2019). Households and nonprofit organizations; net worth, level. FRED Economic Data. https://fred .stlouisfed.org/series/TNWBSHNO

103   by selling something or borrowing money.: Bahney, A. (2018, May 22). 40% of Americans can't cover a $400 emergency expense. CNN

Business. https://money.cnn.com/2018/05/22/pf/emergency-expenses
-household-finances/index.html

104   "almost always wasteful and inefficient.": Pew Research Center. (2015,
November 23). Beyond Distrust: How Americans View Their Government.
http://www.people-press.org/2015/11/23/2-general-opinions-about-the
-federal-government/

104– state, local, and federal governments.: U.S. Bureau of Labor Statistics.
105   (2017, October 24). Employment by major industry sector. https://www
.bls.gov/emp/tables/employment-by-major-industry-sector.htm

105   who own things at the expense of labor.: The Economist. (2013, October
31). Labour pains - Workers share of national income. http://www.economist
.com/news/finance-and-economics/21588900-all-around-world-labour
-losing-out-capital-labour-pains

105   profits going to labor declined from 82.3% to 75.5%: Bivens, J. (2015,
September 10). The decline in labor's share of corporate income since
2000 means $535 billion less for workers. Economic Policy Institute. https://
www.epi.org/publication/the-decline-in-labors-share-of-corporate-income
-since-2000-means-535-billion-less-for-workers/

105   $3,770 less for every worker.: Ibid.

105   tax savings toward increasing their payroll.: Fuhrmans, V. (2018,
October 2). Tax cuts provide limited boost to workers' wages. *Wall Street
Journal*. https://www.wsj.com/articles/tax-cuts-provide-limited-boost-to
-workers-wages-1538472600

105   "all those other forms that have been tried.": Churchill, W. (1947,
November 11). The worst form of government. International Churchill
Society. https://winstonchurchill.org/resources/quotes/the-worst-form
-of-government/

106   enables people to meet their full potential.: James, K. (2018, October 26).
Socialism vs. capitalism: One clear winner. The Heritage Foundation.
https://www.heritage.org/international-economies/commentary/socialism
-vs-capitalism-one-clear-winner

106   opinion of socialism than they did capitalism.: Langlois, S. (2018,
October 23). A growing number of millennials favor socialism over
capitalism. *MarketWatch*. https://www.marketwatch.com/story/ban
-billionaires-capitalism-takes-a-beating-at-the-hands-of-teen-vogue-and
-others-2018-10-18

107   The figure has now doubled to 5.2%.: Greeley, B. (2016, December 16).
Mapping the Growth of Disability Claims in America. *Bloomberg*. https://
www.bloomberg.com/news/features/2016-12-16/mapping-the-growth-of
-disability-claims-in-america

108   commuting to adjacent communities.: Hendrickson, C., Muro, M. and
Galston, W. (2018, November). Countering the geography of discontent:
Strategies for left-behind places. The Brookings Institution. https://www
.brookings.edu/research/countering-the-geography-of-discontent-strategies
-for-left-behind-places/

108   34% of all nonworking men ages 25–54.: Appelbaum, B. (2015, February
28). Out of trouble, but criminal records keep men out of work. *New York
Times*. https://www.nytimes.com/2015/03/01/business/out-of-trouble-but
-criminal-records-keep-men-out-of-work.html

108   failed to live up to their potential.: Muhlhausen, D. (2017, March 14). So
far, federal job-training programs have been outright failures. *The Hill*.
http://thehill.com/blogs/pundits-blog/economy-budget/323885-thus
-far-federal-job-training-programs-have-been-an

109 a quarter of their income on childcare.: Wolfson, A. (2018, July 30). Child care costs are at an all-time high. *New York Post*. https://nypost.com /2018/07/30/child-care-costs-are-at-an-all-time-high/

109 four-year college has tripled in the last 30 years,: Dennin, J. (2018, March 19). Why average costs of living are increasing in the US – and 5 ways to live better for less. Mic.com. https://mic.com/articles/188498/average -cost-of-living-increase-us-2018-calculator-best-cities-health-care-education #.gk0ngFqdz

109 $30 billion in tax preferences in 2017.: Federal Aid for Postsecondary Students. (2018, June 27). Congressional Budget Office. https://www .cbo.gov/publication/53736

109 dollar of subsidized loans they receive.: Canceling Student-Loan Debt Is a Bad Idea. (2019, April 30). *Wall Street Journal*. https://www.wsj.com /articles/canceling-student-loan-debt-is-a-bad-idea-11556663548?mod =hp_opin_pos2

109– a certain share of the graduates' income.: Dynarski, S. (2016, July 9).

110 America can fix its student loan crisis. Just ask Australia. *New York Times*. https://www.nytimes.com/2016/07/10/upshot/america-can-fix-its-student -loan-crisis-just-ask-australia.html

110 outpacing the growth of faculty or students.: New England Center for Investigative Reporting (2014, February 6). New Analysis Shows Problematic Boom In Higher Ed Administrators. *Huffington Post*. https:// www.huffpost.com/entry/higher-ed-administrators-growth_n_4738584

110 students lose access to federal student loans.: Ma, R. (2018, May 29). How The Federal Government Could Control College Costs. *Forbes*. https:// www.forbes.com/sites/rogerma/2018/05/29/how-the-federal-government -could-control-college-costs/#11049a921dcc

110 their degree within six years of enrolling.: Hess, A. (2017, October 10). Bill Gates: US college dropout rates are 'tragic'. CNBC. https://www.cnbc .com/2017/10/10/bill-gates-us-college-dropout-rates-are-tragic.html

110 lay off employees during tough times.: National Center for Employee Ownership. (2019). The economic power of employee ownership. https://www.esopinfo.org/infographics/economic-power-of-employee -ownership.php

112 disadvantaged areas, with the following ideas: Wiens, J. and Jackson, C. (2015, September 13). The importance of young firms for economic growth. Ewing Marion Kauffman Foundation. https://www.kauffman.org/what -we-do/resources/entrepreneurship-policy-digest/the-importance-of -young-firms-for-economic-growth

113 than any time in the last 40 years.: Cohen, P. (2018, July 13). Paychecks lag as profits soar, and prices erode wage gains. *New York Times*. https:// www.nytimes.com/2018/07/13/business/economy/wages-workers-profits .html

113 "major tax cut for middle-income people.": Mason, J. (2018, October 20). Trump says team working on tax cut for middle-income earners. Reuters. https://www.reuters.com/article/us-usa-trump-taxcuts/trump-says-team -working-on-tax-cut-for-middle-income-earners-idUSKCN1MU0X2

115 private sector jobs to work for the government?: Ip, G. (2018, May 2). The problem with a federal jobs guarantee (Hint: It's not the price tag). *Wall Street Journal*. https://www.wsj.com/articles/the-problem-with-a-federal -jobs-guarantee-hint-its-not-the-price-tag-1525267192

117 US could be disrupted by automation.: Muro, M., Maxim, R. and Whiton, J. (2019, January). Automation and artificial intelligence. The

Brookings Institution. https://www.brookings.edu/wp-content/uploads
/2019/01/2019.01_BrookingsMetro_Automation-AI_Report_Muro-Maxim
-Whiton-FINAL-version.pdf

117   adults in 1970 made more than their parents.: Krause, E. and Sawhill, I.
       (2018, June). Seven reasons to worry about the American middle class.
       The Brookings Institution. https://www.brookings.edu/blog/social
       -mobility-memos/2018/06/05/seven-reasons-to-worry-about-the-american
       -middle-class/

9. IMMIGRATION

119   needed to fix our immigration system.: Manchester, J. (2018, December
       11). Majority say they support immigration compromise, poll shows.
       The Hill. https://thehill.com/hilltv/what-americas-thinking/420799
       -majority-say-they-support-immigration-compromise
120   jumped 70% between 2017 and 2018 to 93,000,: Nixon, R. (2018,
       December 10). Asylum Claims Jump Despite Trump's Attempt to Limit
       Immigration. *New York Times.* https://www.nytimes.com/2018/12/10/us
       /politics/trump-asylum-border-.html
121   "both a border security and humanitarian crisis.": Flores, A. (2019,
       March 5). A Record Number of Migrant Families are Showing Up At The
       US-Mexico Border. BuzzFeed News. https://www.buzzfeednews.com
       /article/adolfoflores/record-migrant-families-border-immigration-increase
121   help get them to the US border.: PBS News Hour (2019, March 9).
       Human smuggling industry cashes in on U.S. asylum-seekers. PBS
       Newshour. https://www.pbs.org/newshour/show/human-smuggling
       -industry-cashes-in-on-u-s-asylum-seekers
121   Deferred Action for Childhood Arrivals (DACA) program: Shah, A.,
       Emmanouilidou, L. (2018, April 25). President Obama created DACA.
       Why won't courts let President Trump end it? Public Radio International.
       https://www.pri.org/stories/2018-04-25/president-obama-created-daca
       -why-wont-courts-let-president-trump-end-it
122   68% of those admitted in 2016 accepted for family-based reasons.: Zong,
       J., Batalova, J., & Hallock, J. (2018, February 8). Frequently Requested
       Statistics on Immigrants and Immigration in the United States. Migration
       Policy Institute. https://www.migrationpolicy.org/article/frequently
       -requested-statistics-immigrants-and-immigration-united-states
122   United States: Ibid.
122   Canada: Canada's immigration targets 2016. (2016, March 20). *The
       Canadian Magazine of Immigration.* http://canadaimmigrants.com/canadas
       -immigration-targets-2016/
122   Australia: 2015–16 at a glance. (2016). Australian Government Department
       of Home Affairs. https://archive.homeaffairs.gov.au/about/reports-
       publications/research-statistics/statistics/year-at-a-glance/2015-16
122   *about one million immigrants arrive in the US each year.*: Lopez, G., Bialik, K.,
       & Radford, J. (2018, November 30). Key findings about U.S. immigrants.
       Pew Research Center. http://www.pewresearch.org/fact-tank/2018/11/30
       /key-findings-about-u-s-immigrants/
123   in the United States as an asylum seeker.: American Immigration Council
       (2018, May 14). Asylum in the United States. https://www.american
       immigrationcouncil.org/research/asylum-united-states
123   setting a fee for asylum applications.: Torbati, Y., Rosenberg, M. (2019,
       April 29). Trump directs officials to toughen asylum rules. Reuters.

https://www.reuters.com/article/us-usa-immigration-asylum/trump
-directs-officials-to-toughen-asylum-rules-idUSKCN1S603M

123   necessary documents, among other things.: U.S. Customs and
       Immigration Services. Naturalization Information. https://www.uscis
       .gov/citizenship/educators/naturalization-information#natz_test

124   US has not increased in the last ten years.: Krogstad, J. M., Passel, J. S., &
       Cohn, D. (2017, April 27). 5 facts about illegal immigration in the U.S.
       Pew Research Center. http://www.pewresearch.org/fact-tank/2017/04
       /27/5-facts-about-illegal-immigration-in-the-u-s/

124   from 3,500,000 to 11,989,297.: Warren, R., & Warren, J. R. (2013, June 1).
       Unauthorized immigration to the United States: Annual estimates and
       components of change, by state, 1990 to 2010. *International Migration Review*
       47(2): 296-329. https://www.ncbi.nlm.nih.gov/pmc/articles/PMC3744247/

124   drugs and extreme violence at home.: U.S. Customs and Border Patrol.
       Nationwide apprehensions by citizenship and sector. https://www.cbp
       .gov/sites/default/files/assets/documents/2018-Jul/usbp-nationwide
       -apps-sector-citizenship-fy07-fy17.pdf

124   Iraq, Syria, and Afghanistan during the same period.: Luhnow, D. (2018,
       September 20). Latin America Is the Murder Capital of the World. *Wall
       Street Journal*. https://www.wsj.com/articles/400-murders-a-day-the-crisis
       -of-latin-america-1537455390

124   Latin America and the Caribbean.: Muggah, R., Aguirre Tobon, K.
       (2018, April). Citizen security in Latin America: Facts and Figures.
       Igarapé Institute. https://igarape.org.br/wp-content/uploads/2018/04
       /Citizen-Security-in-Latin-America-Facts-and-Figures.pdf

125   there were unauthorized border crossers.: Gonzalez, R. (2019, January
       16). For 7th consecutive year, visa overstays exceeded illegal border
       crossings. NPR.org. https://www.npr.org/2019/01/16/686056668/for
       -seventh-consecutive-year-visa-overstays-exceeded-illegal-border-crossings

125   apprehended at the US-Canada border.: Ainsley, J. (2019, January 7).
       Only six immigrants in terrorism database stopped by CBP at southern
       border from October to March. NBC News. https://www.nbcnews.com
       /politics/immigration/only-six-immigrants-terrorism-database-stopped
       -cbp-southern-border-first-n955861https://www.nbcnews.com/politics
       /immigration/only-six-immigrants-terrorism-database-stopped-cbp
       -southern-border-first-n955861

125   available nationwide to handle them.: Miroff, N., Sacchetti, M. (2019,
       May 1). Burgeoning court backlog of more than 850,000 cases undercuts
       Trump immigration agenda. *Washington Post*. https://www.washington
       post.com/immigration/burgeoning-court-backlog-of-more-than-850000
       -cases-undercuts-trump-immigration-agenda/2019/05/01/09c0b84a
       -6b69-11e9-a66d-a82d3f3d96d5_story.html?utm_term=.6dfc753ff491

125   59% of all undocumented immigrants in the US: Krogstad, J. M., Passel,
       J. S., & Cohn, D., 5 facts about illegal immigration in the U.S.

125   in fifteen states grew by at least 15%.: American Immigration Council.
       (2017, October 6). Immigrants in West Virginia. https://www.american
       immigrationcouncil.org/research/immigrants-west-virginia

126   at the fastest rate in a decade.: Editorial Board (2019, May 3). Growth
       and the Working Class. *Wall Street Journal*. https://www.wsj.com/articles
       /growth-and-the-working-class-11556920504

126   the economic boost it once did.: Kopf, D. (2017, March 31). US
       productivity growth is negative and economists aren't sure why. *Quartz*.
       https://qz.com/946675/us-productivity-growth-was-negative-in-2016
       -and-economists-arent-sure-why/

126   slowing down for a simple reason: Toossi, M. (2002, May). A century of change: the U.S. labor force, 1950-2050. Bureau of Labor Statistics. https://www.bls.gov/opub/mlr/2002/05/art2full.pdf

126   now half what it was 50 years ago.: The World Bank. Fertility rate, total (births per woman). https://data.worldbank.org/indicator/SP.DYN .TFRT.IN?locations=DE-JP-US

126   at the slowest rate since the 1930s.: Chokshi, N. (2016, December 22). Growth of U.S. Population Is at Slowest Pace Since 1937. *New York Times.* https://www.nytimes.com/2016/12/22/us/usa-population-growth.html

126   as likely to start a business as native-born Americans.: Ivanova, I. (2017, February 10). Immigrants' impact on the U.S. economy in 7 charts. CBS News. https://www.cbsnews.com/news/immigrants-impact-on-the-u-s -economy-in-7-charts/

126    $1 billion or more today were founded by immigrants,: Koh, Y. (2016, March 17). Study: Immigrants founded 51% of U.S. billion-dollar startups. *Wall Street Journal.* https://blogs.wsj.com/digits/2016/03/17 /study-immigrants-founded-51-of-u-s-billion-dollar-startups/

127   services like housekeeping and gardening.: Cortes, P. (2008, June). The effect of low-skilled immigration on U.S. prices: Evidence from CPI data. *Journal of Political Economy* 116(3). https://www.journals.uchicago.edu /doi/abs/10.1086/589756?journalCode=jpe&

127   wage drop for low-skilled Americans by 3–4%.: Borjas, G. (2003). The labor demand curve is downward sloping: Reexamining the impact of immigration on the labor market. *The Quarterly Journal of Economics* 118(4): 1335-1374. http://www.jstor.org/stable/25053941

127   other crimes than are native-born Americans.: Ingraham, C. (2018, June 19). Two charts demolish the notion that immigrants here illegally commit more crime. *Washington Post.* https://www.washingtonpost.com/news /wonk/wp/2018/06/19/two-charts-demolish-the-notion-that-immigrants -here-illegally-commit-more-crime/?utm_term=.4ffb6955868c

127   a fatal crash than licensed ones.: Griffin, L. I., & DeLaZerda, S. (2000, June). Unlicensed to kill. AAA Foundation for Traffic Safety. http:// citeseerx.ist.psu.edu/viewdoc/download?doi=10.1.1.610.9773&rep=rep 1&type=pdf

127   many of them to drive without safety training.: Mendoza, G. (2016, November 30). States offering driver's licenses to immigrants. National Conference of State Legislatures. http://www.ncsl.org/research /immigration/states-offering-driver-s-licenses-to-immigrants.aspx

127   immigrants produced nearly 25% of births in 2015.: The Economist. (2017, August 30). Immigrants boost America's birth rate. https://www .economist.com/graphic-detail/2017/08/30/immigrants-boost-americas -birth-rate

128    $4 trillion over the next 75.: Camarota, S. A., & Zeigler, K. (2016, October 3). A profile of the foreign-born using 2014 and 2015 Census Bureau data. https://cis.org/Report/Immigrants-United-States; The Wall Street Journal. (2013, June 2). A $4.6 trillion opportunity. https://www.wsj .com/articles/SB10001424127887324659404578503172929165846

128   falling on local health care systems: Conover, C. (2018, February). How American citizens finance $18.5 billion in healthcare for unauthorized immigrants. *Forbes.* https://www.forbes.com/sites/theapothecary/2018 /02/26/how-american-citizens-finance-health-care-for-undocumented -immigrants/#66b6cf9a12c4

128   each year at a cost of $400 million.: Radnofsky, L. (2016, March 24). Illegal immigrants get public health care, despite federal policy. *Wall*

Street Journal. https://www.wsj.com/articles/illegal-immigrants-get-public -health-care-despite-federal-policy-1458850082

128   Houston received care funded by charity.: Ibid.

128   1.5 million adult immigrant residents without insurance by 2019.: Ibid.

128   local taxes undocumented immigrants pay each year.: Gee, L. C., Gardner, M., Hill, M. E., & M. W. (2017, March). Undocumented immigrants' state & local tax contributions. Institute on Taxation & Economic Policy. https://itep.org/wp-content/uploads/immigration 2017.pdf

128   never collect benefits due to their status.: Porter, E. (2005, March 5). Illegal immigrants are bolstering Social Security with billions. *New York Times*. https://www.nytimes.com/2005/04/05/business/illegal-immigrants -are-bolstering-social-security-with-billions.html

128   dedicated to regulating our borders and interior.: American Immigration Council. (2017, January 25). The cost of immigration enforcement and border security. https://www.americanimmigration council.org/research/the-cost-of-immigration-enforcement-and-border -security

129   only 703 miles of fencing have been installed.: Federation for American Immigration Reform. (2017, January). The current state of the border fence. https://www.fairus.org/sites/default/files/2017-11/Current _State_Border_Fence.pdf

129   Native American and private land, and a national park.: Trumble, S., & Kasai, N. (2017, October 31). The state of the Southern Border. Third Way. https://www.thirdway.org/memo/the-state-of-the-southern-border

129   technology to share information and intelligence.: U.S. Department of Homeland Security. (2017, May 1). DHS tracking of visa overstays is hindered by insufficient technology. https://www.oig.dhs.gov/sites /default/files/assets/2017/OIG-17-56-May17_0.pdf

129   collaborate on identification, detention, and deportation.: Pew Charitable Trusts. (2015, February 6). Immigration enforcement along U.S. borders and at ports of entry. http://www.pewtrusts.org/en/research -and-analysis/issue-briefs/2015/02/immigration-enforcement-along-us -borders-and-at-ports-of-entry

129   sharing with local and government officials.: National Conference of State Legislatures. (2018, February 12). 2017 immigration report. http:// www.ncsl.org/research/immigration/2017-immigration-report.aspx

129   ranges between $15 and $25 billion.: Nichols, C. (2017, April 28). Would Trump's border wall cost the same as one and a half U.S. aircraft carriers? PolitiFact. https://www.politifact.com/california/statements /2017/apr/28/scott-peters/would-trumps-border-wall-cost-same-one -and-half-us/

129   proposed wall would cost only $145 million.: Jain, R. (2017, January 26). Trump's Mexico border wall: Alternative surveillance methods and countries using them. *International Business Times*. https://www.ibtimes .com/trumps-mexico-border-wall-alternative-surveillance-methods -countries-using-them-2481587

130   Nine hundred of them are serving in the US military.: Gomez, A. (2018, February 13). Who are the DACA DREAMers and how many are here? *USA Today*. https://www.usatoday.com/story/news/politics/2018/02/13 /who-daca-dreamers-and-how-many-here/333045002/

130   Dreamers remain in limbo.: National Immigration Law Center (2018, August). Frequently asked questions, USCIS is accepting DACA renewal

applications. https://www.nilc.org/issues/daca/faq-uscis-accepting-daca
-renewal-applications/

131 the federal government should eliminate ICE.: Shepard, S. (2018, July
11). Poll: Voters oppose abolishing ICE. *Politico.* https://www.politico
.com/story/2018/07/11/immigration-ice-abolish-poll-708703

131 according to several polls taken in 2018.: Mehta, D. (2018, June 19).
Separating families at the border is really unpopular. *FiveThirtyEight.*
https://fivethirtyeight.com/features/separating-families-at-the-border-is
-really-unpopular/

131 High Wall, Big Gate: Friedman, T. L. (2018, November 27). We need a
high wall and a big gate. *New York Times.* https://www.nytimes.com/2018
/11/27/opinion/immigration-republicans-democrats-climate-change
.html

133 which would include the following features: Ideal Immigration. www
.idealimmigration.us

135 US-Mexico family unit border apprehensions.: Ingold, D., Whiteaker, C.,
Rojanasakul, M., Recht, H., & Halford, D. (2017, December 11). Here's
What We Know About Trump's Mexico Wall. *Bloomberg.* https://www.
bloomberg.com/graphics/2017-trump-mexico-wall/how-many
-people-currently-cross/

136 with many seeking asylum.: Specia, M. (2019, April 2). Trump Wants to
Cut Aid to Central America. Here Are Some of the Dozens of U.S.-
Funded Programs. *New York Times.* https://www.nytimes.com/2019/04
/02/world/americas/trump-funding-central-america.html

137 "wondering why your disease has spread a year later.": Stavridis, J.(@
stavridisj) (2019, March 30). https://twitter.com/stavridisj

137 significantly reduce violence in some communities.: United States
Agency for International Development (2019, May 7). Elsalvador –
Overview. https://www.usaid.gov/el-salvador/overview

138 pushed several policies to make legal immigration harder.: Galioto, K.
(2019, February 5). Trump ad-libs that he wants legal immigrants in 'the
largest numbers ever.' *Politico.* https://www.politico.com/story/2019/02
/05/trump-state-of-the-union-legal-immigration-1148629

138 would you take a similar deal today?: Kapur, S. & Dennis, S. T. (2018,
December 13). How Trump let his goal of building a border wall slip
away. *Bloomberg.* https://www.bloomberg.com/news/articles/2018-12-13
/how-trump-let-his-goal-of-building-a-border-wall-slip-away

138 What do you say to that?: Wexler, C. (2017, March 6). Police chiefs across
the country support sanctuary cities because they keep crime down. *LA
Times.* https://www.latimes.com/opinion/op-ed/la-oe-wexler-sanctuary
-cities-immigration-crime-20170306-story.html

140 Nancy Pelosi were calling the wall "immoral.": Zorn, E. (2019, January
11). Pelosi says border walls are 'immoral.' But that's not the conversation
we need to be having right now. *Chicago Tribune.* https://www.chicago
tribune.com/news/opinion/zorn/ct-perspec-zorn-nancy-pelosi-says
-border-walls-are-immoral-but-that-s-not-the-conversation-we-need-to-be
-having-20190111-story.html

10. THE MAGIC MONEY TREE

144 "provides for everything that people want.": Dearden, L. (2017, June 3).
Theresa May prompts anger after telling nurse who hasn't had pay rise
for eight years: 'There's no magic money tree.' *The Independent.* https://

www.independent.co.uk/news/uk/politics/theresa-may-nurse-magic
-money-tree-bbcqt-question-time-pay-rise-eight-years-election-latest
-a7770576.html

144    $1 trillion more than it receives from tax revenues.: Long, H. (2018,
       April 9). Why America's return to $1 trillion deficits is a big problem for
       you. *Washington Post.* https://www.washingtonpost.com/news/wonk/wp
       /2018/04/09/why-americas-return-to-1-trillion-deficits-is-a-big-problem
       -for-you/?utm_term=.f5719f1b0f19

145   same question in the affirmative just five years ago.: Oliphant, B. (2019,
       February 20). Fewer Americans view deficit reduction as a top priority
       as the nation's red ink increases. Pew Research Center. http://www.
       pewresearch.org/fact-tank/2019/02/20/fewer-americans-view-deficit
       -reduction-as-a-top-priority-as-the-nations-red-ink-increases/

145   interest rates soaring, and our economy collapsing.: Ibid.

145   "He won't tell you. I just did.": Mondale, W. (1984, July 20). Transcript
       of Mondale accepting party nomination. *New York Times.* https://www.
       nytimes.com/1984/07/20/us/transcript-of-mondale-address-accepting
       -party-nomination.html

145   Reagan in that November's election.: 1984 Presidential Election. 270towin
       .com. https://www.270towin.com/1984_Election/

145   scary debt pie charts and bar graphs.: Wolf, R. (2012, October 1). Perot's
       economic stance resonates 20 years later. *USA Today.* https://www.usatoday
       .com/story/news/nation/2012/10/01/perot-20-years-later/1603897/

145   He lost every state.: Malice, M. (2016, July 12). Why third-party
       candidates can't win. *The Observer.* https://observer.com/2016/07/why
       -third-party-candidates-cant-win/

146    $16.1 trillion as of December 31, 2018.: U.S. Department of the Treasury.
       (2018, November 19). Federal debt held by the public. https://fred.stlouis
       fed.org/series/FYGFDPUN

146    $1 trillion by the end of 2019.: Henney, M. (2019, January 2). How high
       U.S. deficit could climb in 2019. FOX Business. https://www.foxbusiness
       .com/economy/how-high-us-deficit-could-climb-in-2019

146   projected to reach $390 billion this year.: Schwartz, N. D. (2018,
       September 25). As debt rises, the government will soon spend more on
       interest than on the military. *New York Times.* https://www.nytimes.com
       /2018/09/25/business/economy/us-government-debt-interest.html

146   the entire budget of the Department of Defense.: Investor's Business
       Daily. (2018, October 16). Go figure: Federal revenues hit all-time highs
       under Trump tax cuts. https://www.investors.com/politics/editorials
       /trump-tax-cuts-federal-revenues-deficits/; Wolf, Z. B. (2018, July 11).
       How much does the U.S. spend on defense? A lot! CNN.com. https://
       www.cnn.com/2018/07/11/politics/trump-defense-spending/index.html

146   it needs to "tighten its belt" just like families do.: Coppola, F. (2018, April
       30). Governments are nothing like households. *Forbes.* https://www
       .forbes.com/sites/francescoppola/2018/04/30/governments-are-nothing
       -like-households/#2f7637b454f8

146   stimulate employment and economic activity.: Ibid.

147   the annual deficit could reach as high as $2 trillion.: Egan, M. & Wiener-
       Bronner, D. (2018, April 15). Trillion-dollar budget deficits will make
       next recession more painful. CNN Business. https://money.cnn.com
       /2018/04/15/investing/stocks-week-ahead-deficit-recession/index.html

147   at almost any time since World War II.: Schulze, E. (2018, July 26). 3
       charts that show why the US should stop ignoring its debt problem.

CNBC. https://www.cnbc.com/2018/07/26/3-charts-that-show-why-the
-us-should-stop-ignoring-its-debt-problem.html

147 increase its debt/GDP over the next five years.: Ibid.

148 every president should seek to reduce or eliminate it.: Committee for a
Responsible Federal Budget. (2015, August 6). Can we solve our debt
situation by cutting waste, fraud, abuse, earmarks, and/or foreign aid?
http://www.crfb.org/blogs/we-can-solve-our-debt-situation-cutting-waste
-fraud-abuse-earmarks-andor-foreign-aid

148 in the context of a $4.1 trillion federal budget.: Ibid.; Peter G. Peterson
Foundation. (2019). Spending. https://www.pgpf.org/finding-solutions
/understanding-the-budget/spending

148 The real figure is less than one percent.: Rutsch, P. (2015, February 10).
Guess how much of Uncle Sam's money goes to foreign aid. Guess again!
NPR.org. http://www.npr.org/sections/goatsandsoda/2015/02/10
/383875581/guess-how-much-of-uncle-sams-money-goes-to-foreign-aid
-guess-again

149 only 31% of all federal spending.: Peter G. Peterson Foundation. (2019).
Spending. https://www.pgpf.org/finding-solutions/understanding-the
-budget/spending

149 Medicare will be unable to do the same by 2026.: Rappeport, A. (2019,
April 22). Social Security and Medicare Funds Face Insolvency, Report
Finds. *New York Times.* https://www.nytimes.com/2019/04/22/us/politics
/social-security-medicare-insolvency.html

150 **chart: Mandatory programs and interest costs will take over more of
the federal budget, squeezing discretionary programs**: Peter G.
Peterson Foundation, Spending.

150 large wage gains that were expected for workers.: Peter G. Peterson
Foundation. (2018, August 8). How have tax cuts affected the economy
and debt? Here's what we know so far. https://www.pgpf.org/blog/2018
/08/how-have-tax-cuts-affected-the-economy-and-debt-heres-what-we
-know-so-far

150 other developed economies around the world.: OECD. (2018, November
20). OECD GDP growth slows to 0.5% in third quarter of 2018. https://
www.oecd.org/economy/gdp-growth-third-quarter-2018-oecd.htm

150 "create additional revenue for the government.": Bryan, B. (2018, August
28). Treasury Secretary Steve Mnuchin doubled down on a claim about
the tax bill that almost every independent group says is wrong. *Business
Insider.* https://www.businessinsider.com/mnuchin-gop-trump-tax-law
-pay-for-itself-deficit-rising-debt-2018-8

150 He is wrong.: Evilsizer, T. (2019, February 19). Putting the 'Trump tax
cuts will pay for themselves' myth to bed. *The Hill.* https://thehill.com
/opinion/finance/430604-putting-the-trump-tax-cuts-will-pay-for
-themselves-myth-to-bed

150 add $1.9 trillion to the national debt through 2027.: Committee for a
Responsible Federal Budget. (2018, September 28). A fiscal year defined
by $2.4 trillion in new debt. http://www.crfb.org/blogs/fiscal-year-defined
-24-trillion-new-debt; The Budget and Economic Outlook: 2018 to 2028.
(2018, April). https://www.cbo.gov/system/files?file=115th-congress-2017
-2018/reports/53651-outlook.pdf#page=133

151 from car and credit card loans to mortgages—more expensive.: Tisch,
A. (2017, July 20). The debt ceiling is dumb -- and dangerous. *CNN.*
https://www.cnn.com/2017/07/20/opinions/the-debt-ceiling-is-dumb
-and-dangerous-opinion-tisch/index.html

152 "debate later whether to pay for it—or not.": Ibid.

152 Simpson-Bowles Deficit Reduction Commission—calls this "chest-pounding fakery.": Long, H. (2018, April 12). The 'balanced-budget amendment is a joke,' says GOP deficit hawk Alan Simpson. *Washington Post.* https://www.washingtonpost.com/news/wonk/wp/2018/04/12 /the-balanced-budget-amendment-is-a-joke-says-famed-gop-deficit-hawk -alan-simpson/?utm_term=.9b01fa528747

153 Ronald Reagan's economic agenda as "voodoo economics.": Serwer, A. (2018, December 2). Former President George H.W. Bush's tortured relationship with economics. Yahoo Finance. https://finance.yahoo.com /news/president-george-h-w-bush-tortured-relationship-economics -175710643.html

153 "borrow in their own currency, I think, is just wrong.": Forsyth, R.W. (2019, March 4). Do budget deficits matter? Not to today's left or right. *Barron's.* https://www.barrons.com/articles/do-u-s-budget-deficits -matter-not-to-todays-left-or-right-51551468212?shareToken=st87786121a 3794142a9018aad0f8ff7e1&mod=e2realclear

154 other studies peg the figure at much less.: Committee for a Responsible Federal Budget. (2015, August 6). Do tax cuts pay for themselves? http:// www.crfb.org/blogs/do-tax-cuts-pay-themselves

155 The Fiscal Responsibility Act could prevent that ratio from exceeding 100%.: Schulze, E. (2018, July 26). 3 charts that show why the US should stop ignoring its debt problem. CNBC. https://www.cnbc.com/2018/07/26 /3-charts-that-show-why-the-us-should-stop-ignoring-its-debt-problem.html

155 not at all since 1997.: Desilver, D. (2018, January 16). Congress has long struggled to pass spending bills on time. Pew Research Center. http:// www.pewresearch.org/fact-tank/2018/01/16/congress-has-long-struggled -to-pass-spending-bills-on-time/

157 from the US Government Accountability Office (GAO): Watchblog (2019, March 28). Did You Know the Government Gets Audited, Too? https://blog.gao.gov/2019/03/28/did-you-know-the-government-gets -audited-too/

157 "accurate, truthful, and complete.": United States Securities and Exchange Commission (2002, June 24). All About Auditors: What Investors Need to Know. https://www.sec.gov/reportspubs/investor-publications/investor pubsaboutauditorshtm.html

159 you said you were the "king of debt" and that you "loved debt.": Egan, M. (2016, May 7). Donald Trump: 'I'm the king of debt.' CNN Business. https://money.cnn.com/2016/05/05/investing/trump-king-of-debt-fire -janet-yellen/index.html

161 45% of all income tax revenue.: Gramm, P. & Solon, M. (2019, March 4). Tax reform unleashed the U.S. economy. *Wall Street Journal.* https://www .wsj.com/articles/tax-reform-unleashed-the-u-s-economy-11551740837

11. GUN SAFETY

165 "I'd never heard it before.": Healy, J., Stack, L. (2019,. May 7). School Shooting Leaves 1 Student Dead and 8 Injured. *New York Times.* https:// www.nytimes.com/2019/05/07/us/colorado-school-shooting.html#click =https://t.co/gpQ2sA9ohf

166 25 Times More Likely to Be Shot and Killed with a Gun than People in Other Developed Countries: Everytown (2019). Learn What It Takes to Keep America Safe. https://everytown.org/learn/

166   the highest level in nearly 40 years.: Howard, J. (2019, December 14).
       Gun deaths in US reach highest level in nearly 40 years, CDC data
       reveal. CNN Health. https://www.cnn.com/2018/12/13/health/gun
       -deaths-highest-40-years-cdc/index.html

166   288 school shootings in the United States since 2009.: Grabow, C, Rose,
       L. (2018, May 21). The US has had 57 times as many school shootings as
       the other major industrialized nations combined. CNN.com. https://
       www.cnn.com/2018/05/21/us/school-shooting-us-versus-world-trnd
       /index.html

166   59% higher than the previous record of 59 in 2006.: Center for Homeland
       Defense and Security K-12 School Shooting Database (2019). Incidents
       by year. https://www.chds.us/ssdb/incidents-by-year/

166   background checks and legal liability for gun manufacturers.: Everytown,
       Learn What It Takes to Keep America Safe.

167   "a bad guy with a gun is a good guy with a gun.": Overby, P. (2012,
       December 21). NRA: 'Only Thing That Stops A Bad Guy With A Gun Is
       A Good Guy With A Gun'. NPR.org. https://www.npr.org/2012/12/21
       /167824766/nra-only-thing-that-stops-a-bad-guy-with-a-gun-is-a-good
       -guy-with-a-gun

167   Their most recent data as of early 2019 found: Gallup (2016). In Depth:
       Guns. Gallup. https://news.gallup.com/poll/1645/guns.aspx

167   A February 2019 Reuters-Ipsos poll found: Lohr, A. A., (2019, February
       8). Reuters/Ipsos Data: American Perceptions on Gun Control
       (02/08/2019). Ipsos. https://www.ipsos.com/en-us/news-polls/reuters
       -ipsos-data-gun-control-2019-02-08

167   which would include gun shows.: Monmouth University Poll (2018, March
       8). Gun Owners Divided on Gun Policy; Parkland Students Having an
       Impact. https://www.monmouth.edu/polling-institute/reports
       /MonmouthPoll_US_030818/

167   over ten percentage points since the 1990s.: PEW Research Center (2017,
       June 22). Public Views About Guns. https://www.people-press.org/2017
       /06/22/public-views-about-guns/#total

168   compared to just 12% of non-gun owners.: Oliphant, J. B., Gramlich, J.
       (2017, October 12). Supporters of stricter gun laws are less likely to
       contact elected officials. Pew Research Center. https://www.pewresearch
       .org/fact-tank/2017/10/12/supporters-of-stricter-gun-laws-are-less-likely
       -to-contact-elected-officials/

168   gun control measures—like banning assault rifles—may not work.:
       Farley, R. (2013, February 1). Did the 1994 Assault Weapons Ban Work?
       FactCheck.org. https://www.factcheck.org/2013/02/did-the-1994-assault
       -weapons-ban-work/

168   "had it been in effect for a longer period.": Farley, Did the 1994 Assault
       Weapons Ban Work?

169   "may be used to advocate or promote gun control.": 104th Congress.
       (1996, September 30). Public Law 104-208. https://www.govinfo.gov
       /content/pkg/PLAW-104publ208/pdf/PLAW-104publ208.pdf

169   "the proper research and kept it going all this time.": Brantley, M. (2015,
       October 6). Jay Dickey regrets his legislation to curb gun research.
       Arkansas Times. https://arktimes.com/arkansas-blog/2015/10/06/jay
       -dickey-regrets-his-legislation-to-curb-gun-research

169   they are responsible for a similar number of deaths.: Gregory, S., Wilson,
       C. (2018, March 22). 6 Real Ways We Can Reduce Gun Violence in America.
       TIME. http://time.com/5209901/gun-violence-america-reduction/

169   the effects of many commonly discussed gun policies.: RAND
       Corporation. What Science Tells Us About the Effects of Gun Policies.
       https://www.rand.org/research/gun-policy/essays/what-science-tells-us
       -about-the-effects-of-gun-policies.html

170   You can even make an AR-15 into a pistol.: Stokes, J. (2016, June 20). Why
       millions of Americans – including me – own the AR-15. Vox.com.
       https://www.vox.com/2016/6/20/11975850/ar-15-owner-orlando

170   print their own weapons and accessories at home.: Levenson, E. (2018,
       August 28). Maker of 3D-printed guns begins selling blueprints, despite
       court order. CNN.com. https://www.cnn.com/2018/08/28/us/3d-printed
       -guns-cody-wilson-blueprint/index.html

170   like New Zealand did in the wake of a 2019 mass shooting: Schwartz, M.
       (2019, April 10). New Zealand Passes Law Banning Most Semi-Automatic
       Weapons. NPR.org. https://www.npr.org/2019/04/10/711820023/new
       -zealand-passes-law-banning-most-semi-automatic-weapons

170   almost six in 10 Americans told Gallup in 2018 that they would reject such
       a ban.: Levenson, Maker of 3D-printed guns begins selling blueprints,
       despite court order.

170   only 3% of gun-related homicides in the US: Federal Bureau of
       Investigation-Uniform Crime Reporting (2013). Crime in the United
       States 2013: Murder Victims. https://ucr.fbi.gov/crime-in-the-u.s/2013
       /crime-in-the-u.s.-2013/offenses-known-to-law-enforcement/expanded
       -homicide/expanded_homicide_data_table_8_murder_victims_by
       _weapon_2009-2013.xls

170–   just 298 homicides in that same year.: Hinkle, A.B. (2018, February 21).
171   Searching for gun violence solutions that don't collectivize punishment.
       Reason. https://reason.com/2018/02/21/searching-for-gun-solutions/

171   accounted for over 6,000 homicides.: Federal Bureau of Investigation-
       Uniform Crime Reporting, Crime in the United States 2013: Murder
       Victims.

171   than people in the United States.: Ingraham, C. (2018, June 19). There
       are more guns than people in the United States, according to a new
       study of global firearm ownership. Washington Post. https://www
       .washingtonpost.com/news/wonk/wp/2018/06/19/there-are-more-guns
       -than-people-in-the-united-states-according-to-a-new-study-of-global
       -firearm-ownership/?utm_term=.ad6effe64efd

171   revolvers handed in by law-abiding citizens.: Horn, D. (2013, January 13).
       Gun buybacks popular but ineffective, experts say. USA Today. https://
       www.usatoday.com/story/news/nation/2013/01/12/gun-buybacks
       -popular-but-ineffective/1829165/

171   often through the infamous "gun show loophole.": Miller, M., Hepburn,
       L., Azrael, D. (2017, February 21). Firearm Acquisition Without
       Background Checks: Results of a National Survey. Annals of Internal
       Medicine. https://annals.org/aim/fullarticle/2595892/firearm-acquisition
       -without-background-checks-results-national-survey

171   "after the gunman passed a federal background check.": Edmondson, C.
       (2019, February 27). A Guide to the House's First Major Gun Control
       Vote in Years. New York Times. https://www.nytimes.com/2019/02/27/us
       /politics/gun-control-bills.html

171   "right of the people to keep and bear arms.": Cornell Law Legal
       Information Institute. Second Amendment.: https://www.law.cornell
       .edu/wex/second_amendment

172   you can't buy a machine gun.: Bureau of Alcohol, Tobacco, Firearms, and Explosives (2019, February 14). National Fire Arms Act. https://www.atf.gov/rules-and-regulations/national-firearms-act

172   you aren't allowed—with a few exceptions—to have a gun at all.: Pavlo, W. (2018, October 5). Ruling Clarifies That Some White-Collar Felons Can Possess A Firearm. *Forbes.* https://www.forbes.com/sites/walter pavlo/2018/10/05/ruling-clarifies-that-some-white-collar-felons-can -possess-a-firearm/

172   repeatedly and recently by the US Supreme Court.: Allen, J. Kruzman, D. (2018, July 24) U.S. appeals court upholds right to carry gun in public. Reuters. https://www.reuters.com/article/us-usa-guns-court/us -appeals-court-upholds-right-to-carry-gun-in-public-idUSKBN1KE28C

172   was never voted on in the House.: Propublica (2013, April 17). Senate Vote 97 – Defeats Manchin-Toomey Background Checks Proposal. https://projects.propublica.org/represent/votes/113/senate/1/97

172–   criminal convictions into the national background check system.:
173   Berman, R. (2018, March 22). Congress's 'Baby Steps' on Guns. *The Atlantic.* https://www.theatlantic.com/politics/archive/2018/03/congress -guns-fix-nics-baby-steps/556250/

173   turn his semiautomatic rifle into a machine gun.: Velshi, A., Watts, W. (2019, March 26). Bump stocks are now illegal in the United States. MSNBC. https://www.msnbc.com/velshi-ruhle/watch/bump-stocks-are -now-illegal-in-the-united-states-1465125443628

173   "the transfer of any firearm to a non-licensed individual.": Bureau of Alcohol, Tobacco, Firearms and Explosives (2015, September 14). Who must comply with the requirements to conduct a NICS background check prior to transferring a firearm? https://www.atf.gov/firearms/qa /who-must-comply-requirements-conduct-nics-background-check-prior -transferring-firearm

173   as well as any criminal history and stays in a mental institution.: Pagliery, J., Smith, A. (2018, February 15). How gun background checks work. CNN.com. https://www.cnn.com/2018/02/15/us/gun-background-checks -florida-school-shooting/index.html

173   obtained through private-party transfers.: Giffords Law Center (2018). Universal Background Checks. https://lawcenter.giffords.org/gun-laws /policy-areas/background-checks/universal-background-checks/

174   fell an astounding 49% between 1993 to 2017.: Gramlich, J. (2019, January 3). 5 facts about crime in the U.S. Pew Research Center. https://www .pewresearch.org/fact-tank/2019/01/03/5-facts-about-crime-in-the-u-s/

174   higher rates of violent crime than in the US: Beauchamp, Z. (2018, February 15). America doesn't have more crime than other rich countries. It just has more guns. Vox.com. https://www.vox.com/2015/8/27/9217163 /america-guns-europe

174   which have much more permissive gun laws.: Asher, J., Nguyen, M. (2017, October 26). Gun Laws Stop At State Lines, But Guns Don't. *FiveThirty-Eight.* https://fivethirtyeight.com/features/gun-laws-stop-at-state-lines -but-guns-dont/

174   the perpetrator was someone who illegally possessed a gun.: Fabio, A., Duelol, J., Creppage, K., O'Donnell, K., Laporte, R. (2016, January 15). Gaps continue in firearm surveillance: Evidence from a large U.S. City Bureau of Police. *Social Medicine.* http://www.socialmedicine.info/index .php/socialmedicine/article/view/852/1649

175 "if you put a gun in their hands, they are more lethal.": Cassidy, J. (2018, March 23). A Glimmer of Hope in the Political Impasse on Gun Control. *New Yorker.* https://www.newyorker.com/news/our-columnists/before -the-march-for-our-lives-a-bit-of-good-news-on-gun-control

175 Senators Richard Blumenthal (D-CT) and Lindsey Graham (R-SC): Killough, A. (2018, March 8). Graham, Blumenthal unveil their own gun restraining order bill. CNN.com. https://www.cnn.com/2018/03/08 /politics/graham-blumenthal-gun-bill/index.html

175 issue these extreme risk protection orders.: Ibid.

175 Jack Reed (D-RI), Bill Nelson (D-FL), and Marco Rubio (R-FL): Rubio, M. (2018, March 22). Rubio, Nelson, Reed Introduce "Red Flag" Bill. https://www.rubio.senate.gov/public/index.cfm/press-releases?Content Record_id=A1C5B7D3-D60C-42E0-BEE9-AAA74B1416D4

175 encourage more states to be able to do the same.: Rubio, M., Nelson, B., Reed, R. (2019, January 3). Extreme Risk Protection Order and Violence Prevention Act. https://www.rubio.senate.gov/public/_cache/files /178fef18-74cb-406f-b9ac-efd4ca51a258/FE66CF63CCF3DF78879B42 CD18981863.extreme-risk-protection-order-and-violence-prevention-act -one-pager-.pdf

175 found at crime scenes and traced to dealers.: Giffords Law Center (2018) Statistics on Gun Trafficking & Private Sales. https://lawcenter.giffords .org/gun-traffickingprivate-sales-statistics/

176 levy heavier fines and suspensions.: Feldman, R. Gerney, A. (2013, December 15). A grand bargain on guns? Here's how. *LA Times.* https:// www.latimes.com/opinion/la-xpm-2013-dec-15-la-oe-feldman-gun -control-bargain-20131215-story.html

176 the age to purchase tobacco raised from 18 to 21.: Ingber, S. (2019, April 19). Anti-Tobacco Advocates Question McConnell Plan To Raise Minimum Purchasing Age. NPR.org. https://www.npr.org/2019/04/19 /715117833/anti-tobacco-advocates-question-mcconnell-plan-to-raise -minimum-purchasing-age

176 buy "long guns" like rifles and shotguns.: Lucey, C., Daly, M. (2018, February 22). Trump endorses raising minimum age to 21 for more weapons. PBS.org. https://www.pbs.org/newshour/politics/trump -endorsees-raising-minimum-age-to-21-for-more-weapons

176 "CDC has the authority to conduct research on the causes of gun violence.": Berman, R. (2018, March 22). Congress's 'Baby Steps' on Guns. *The Atlantic.* https://www.theatlantic.com/politics/archive/2018 /03/congress-guns-fix-nics-baby-steps/556250/

177 prohibited juvenile offender to possess a firearm.: Editorial Staff (2018, February 15). Editorial: Bill aims to disarm serious juvenile offenders. *Omaha World-Herald.* https://www.omaha.com/opinion/editorial-bill -aims-to-disarm-serious-juvenile-offenders/article_f9df05b4-2b53-5973 -9122-39c5f471f157.html

177 committed to a mental health facility from buying weapons.: Tyree, E., Beal, K. (2018, February 16). Local senators talk mental health, firearms in Richmond. ABC 13-WSET News. https://wset.com/news/at-the-capitol /local-senators-talk-mental-health-firearms-in-richmond

177 "knowingly and intentionally" provide a firearm to a felon.: Prabhu, M. (2018, February 5). Bill to keep guns out of felons' hands advances in Georgia House. *Atlanta Journal-Constitution.* https://www.ajc.com/news /state--regional-govt--politics/bill-keep-guns-out-felons-hands-advances -georgia-house/4aRwBrnOrn3GNA5QivzrPJ/

177   purchase a firearm and fails a background check.: Everytown for Gun Safety (2018, April 25). Tennessee Moms Demand Action, Everytown applaud Signing of Bill to Keep Guns Away From People With Dangerous Mental Illnesses. https://everytown.org/press/tennessee-moms-demand -action-everytown-applaud-signing-of-bill-to-keep-guns-away-from-people -with-dangerous-mental-illnesses/

177   authority to seize weapons from domestic abusers.: Gagliano, K. (2018, April 25). Domestic violence firearms limitations advances. *The Advocate.* https://www.theadvocate.com/baton_rouge/news/politics/legislature /article_27f9736e-48de-11e8-bab5-ab5b2e8c5ff5.html

178   Here is his proposal: Stokes, J. (2018, April 28). A Gun Nut's Guide to Gun Control That Works. *Politico.* https://www.politico.com/magazine /story/2018/04/28/gun-nuts-guide-to-gun-control-federal-semi-automatic -firearm-license-218072

12. FIXING THE SYSTEM

188   26 out of 32 developed nations in citizen voting share.: Desilver, D. (2018, May 21). U.S. trails most developed countries in voter turnout. Pew Research Center. http://www.pewresearch.org/fact-tank/2018/05 /21/u-s-voter-turnout-trails-most-developed-countries/

189   still under 20% of all registered voters.: Desilver, D. (2018, October 3). Turnout in this year's U.S. House primaries rose sharply, especially on the Democratic side. Pew Research Center. http://www.pewresearch.org /fact-tank/2018/10/03/turnout-in-this-years-u-s-house-primaries-rose -sharply-especially-on-the-democratic-side/

189   **chart: US House of Representative Seats 1997–2016**: Cillizza, C. (2017, April 7). This is the most amazing chart on Congress you'll see today. CNN.com. https://www.cnn.com/2017/04/07/politics/house-swing-seats -congress/index.html

190   just 9% of the entire country.: Parlapiano, A. & Pearce, A. (2016, August 1). Only 9% of America chose Trump and Clinton as the nominees. *New York Times.* https://www.nytimes.com/interactive/2016/08/01/us/elections /nine-percent-of-america-selected-trump-and-clinton.html

190   324,000,000: Ibid.

191   Republicans increasingly prefer to live alongside Republicans.: Enten, H. (2018, January 26). Ending gerrymandering won't fix what ails America. *FiveThirtyEight.* https://fivethirtyeight.com/features/ending-gerry mandering-wont-fix-what-ails-america/

192   **chart: Votes for Supreme Court Justices**: Loesche, D. (2018, June 28). Votes for Supreme Court justices. Statista. https://www.statista.com/chart /14477/votes-for-us-supreme-court-justice-since-1986/

193   judges can stay on the bench as long as they'd like.: Lafrance, A. (2013, November 12). Lifetime appointments don't make sense anymore. Slate. https://slate.com/technology/2013/11/lifetime-appointments-dont-make -sense-anymore.html

193   Supreme Court nominees have been getting younger.: Ingold, D. (2017, April 7). Eighty is the new 70 as Supreme Court justices serve longer and longer. *Bloomberg.* https://www.bloomberg.com/graphics/2017-supreme -court-justice-tenure/

193   end to lifetime appointments to the Supreme Court.: Hurley, L. (2015, July 20). Americans favor Supreme Court term limits: Reuters/Ipsos poll . Reuters. https://www.reuters.com/article/us-usa-court-poll-idUSKCN 0PU09820150720

193   "greater degree of turnover among the judges.": Broder, J.M. & Marshall, C. (2005, July 30). White House memos offer opinion on Supreme Court. *New York Times*. http://query.nytimes.com/gst/fullpage.html?res =9A0CE5DA113FF933A05754C0A9639C8B63

193   limit Supreme Court justices to a single 18-year term.: Fix the Court. Term limits. https://fixthecourt.com/fix/term-limits/

194   the last one happened over 25 years ago.: Levy, M. (2010, September 23). Twenty-seventh Amendment. *Encyclopaedia Britannica*. https://www .britannica.com/topic/Twenty-seventh-Amendment

195   **chart: Percent Upset at Marriage to Member of Other Party**: Mooney, C. (2012, October 1). Why Republicans don't want to marry Democrats. *Psychology Today*. https://www.psychologytoday.com/us/blog/your-brain -politics/201210/why-republicans-don-t-want-marry-democrats

195   "even revive the American dream.": Cohen, R. (2017, March 4). Travel abroad, in your own country. *New York Times*. https://www.nytimes.com /2017/03/04/opinion/sunday/travel-abroad-in-your-own-country.html

196   "they can be trusted with their own government.": Jefferson, T. (1789, January 8). Thomas Jefferson to Richard Price. Library of Congress. https://www.loc.gov/exhibits/jefferson/60.html

196   thought Judge Judy was on the Supreme Court.: Shaw, M. (2017, May 25). Civic Illiteracy in America. *Harvard Political Review*. http://harvardpolitics .com/culture/civic-illiteracy-in-america/

196   only 26% of Americans can name all three branches of government.: Shapiro, S., Brown, C. (2018, February 21). A Look at Civics Education in the United States. American Federation of Teachers. https://www.aft.org /ae/summer2018/shapiro_brown

196   12% believe the Bill of Rights includes the right to own a pet.: Annenberg Public Policy Center (2015, September 16). Is There a Constitutional Right to Own a Home or a Pet? https://www.annenbergpublicpolicy center.org/is-there-a-constitutional-right-to-own-a-home-or-a-pet/

196   only 30% believed the Constitution to be the supreme law of the land.: Newsweek Staff (2011, March 20). Take the Quiz: What We Don't Know. *Newsweek*. https://www.newsweek.com/take-quiz-what-we-dont-know -66047

196   57% of Americans could not name a single Supreme Court Justice.: C-Span (2017, March 17). C-Span/PSB Supreme Court Survey 2017. https://www.c-span.org/scotussurvey2017/

196   "proficient" on the 2010 National Assessment of Educational Progress civics test.: Shapiro, S., Brown, C., A Look at Civics Education in the United States. https://www.aft.org/ae/summer2018/shapiro_brown

196   the other 11 states have no civics requirement.: Shaw, M., Civic Illiteracy in America.

197   only 18% required students to take a course in American history or government.: Ibid.

197   But then Congress zeroed out the funding entirely.: Silverbrook, J. (2015, September 8). The crisis in civic education funding. *Washington Times*. https://www.washingtontimes.com/news/2015/sep/8/constitutional -literacy-the-crisis-in-civic-educat/

197   "I will mount the usual weekly cross and let you drive the nails.": Dickinson, M. (2009, February 10). A Primer on Presidential Press Conferences. *Presidential Power* (blog). https://sites.middlebury.edu /presidentialpower/2009/02/10/a-primer-on-presidential-press -conferences/

197   presidents have averaged only about two a month.: The American
       Presidency Project (2018, March 20). Presidential News Conferences.
       https://www.presidency.ucsb.edu/statistics/data/presidential-news
       -conferences

197   President Trump had only one solo news conference.: Ibid.

200   over 100 times in a single session of Congress.: Terbush, J. (2014, April
       30). The rise of the filibuster, in one maddening chart. *The Week*. https://
       theweek.com/speedreads/454162/rise-filibuster-maddening-chart

200   presidential contenders have suggested getting rid of it entirely.: Chait, J.
       (2018, December 21). Trump Wants to End the Filibuster. He's Right.
       New York Magazine. http://nymag.com/intelligencer/2018/12/trump-end
       -filibuster-senate-right.html

201   complete each year by the end of its fiscal year.: Desilver, D. (2018,
       January 16). Congress has long struggled to pass spending bills on time.
       Pew Research Center. http://www.pewresearch.org/fact-tank/2018/01
       /16/congress-has-long-struggled-to-pass-spending-bills-on-time/

201   budgeting and appropriations process "irreparably broken.": Bolton, A.
       (2018, April 17). Budget chairman floats plan to eliminate his own
       committee. *The Hill*. https://thehill.com/homenews/senate/383454
       -budget-chairman-floats-plan-to-eliminate-his-own-committee

201   Congress banned earmarks in 2011.: Rollcall Staff (2014, June 30). The
       Congressional Earmark Ban: the Real Bridge to Nowhere | Commentary.
       https://www.rollcall.com/news/the_congressional_earmark_ban_the
       _real_bridge_to_nowhere_commentary-235380-1.html

201   a tool for building support for difficult bills.: Grumet, J. (2018, March 5).
       Opinion: Want to Fix the Debt? Bring Back Earmarks. Roll Call. https://
       www.rollcall.com/news/opinion/want-fix-debt-bring-back-earmarks

202   the national capital (the District of Columbia) for the South.: Hamilton,
       A. (1790, June). The Dinner Table Bargain. PBS.org. https://www.pbs
       .org/wgbh/americanexperience/features/hamilton-dinner-table-bargain
       -june-1790/

203   build new coalitions [and] forge new solutions.": Fallert, N. (2019,
       February 5). President Trump's State of the Union address: transcript.
       Vox.com. https://www.vox.com/2019/2/5/18212533/president-trump
       -state-of-the-union-address-live-transcript

203   "the enemy of the people.": Grynbaum, M. (2017, February 7). Trump
       calls the news media the 'enemy of the people'. *New York Times*. https://
       www.nytimes.com/2017/02/17/business/trump-calls-the-news-media
       -the-enemy-of-the-people.html

203   Democrats in Congress "hate our country.": Hains, T. (2019, March 4).
       Trump: "We have people in our Congress who hate our country".
       RealClearPolitics. https://www.realclearpolitics.com/video/2019/03/04
       /trump_we_have_people_in_congress_who_hate_our_country.html

205   61% of Democrats thought Republicans were racist, sexist, or bigoted.:
       Hart, K. (2018, November 12). Exclusive poll: most Democrats see
       Republicans as racist, sexist. Axios. https://www.axios.com/poll
       -democrats-and-republicans-hate-each-other-racist-ignorant-evil-99ae7afc
       -5a51-42be-8ee2-3959e43ce320.html

ACKNOWLEDGMENTS

Many people contributed to the creation of this book. We'd like to thank Nancy Jacobson for her tireless work in founding and building No Labels into the inspiring movement it has become. Since its inception, No Labels has benefited from the volunteer contributions of policy thinkers like Bill Galston and Clarine Nardi Riddle, the editing expertise of Warren Wheat, and the advice of political leaders like our national chairman Senator Joe Lieberman and advisors like Senator Evan Bayh and Representative Tom Davis. We benefited from the fresh thinking of the New Center policy team and from the guidance of the team at Diversion Books, in particular our editor Melanie Madden and publisher Scott Waxman. Finally, we received valuable input into early drafts of this book from No Labels citizen leaders across the country. Thank you all.

A PERSONAL NOTE FROM RYAN

Mom and Dad: Thank you for always being there. Erika: You sacrifice a lot so I can do this work. Through my early mornings, late nights and time away from home, you are the glue that holds our family together. I appreciate it more than you know and I love you. Elle: I may be a writer but I can't put into words what it meant when you came into our life. Daddy loves you so much.

A PERSONAL NOTE FROM MARGARET

Nancy, thank you for always believing in me and your tireless pursuit to better our democracy. Matt, thank you for being my rock and constant source of inspiration. Mom and Dad, thank you for raising me to believe anything is possible. To all the talented staff and amazing volunteer leaders across the country who have worked so hard to put these principles of problem solving above all for the future of this great nation, we are forever grateful. You've touched my life in remarkable ways. This is truly a movement of the people and I am so proud to be a part of it.

INDEX

Note: Page references in *italics* refer to figures.

ABOUT THE AUTHORS

RYAN CLANCY is a senior advisor for No Labels, where he leads the development of policy and communications for the organization. He is an experienced strategist who has advised leaders and crafted messages at the highest levels of business, government, and philanthropy.

Ryan has helped some of the world's most respected leaders and organizations tell their story: serving as a speechwriter for cabinet officials in the Obama administration; ghostwriting books; developing corporate narratives and executive positioning plans for Fortune 500 companies and CEOs and investor pitches for start-up companies and entrepreneurs; and advising political reform groups and candidates on all facets of communications strategy.

A graduate of Villanova University, Ryan lives in Brooklyn with his wife Erika and daughter Elle.

MARGARET WHITE began her political career helping good people get elected to public office, serving on three senatorial and gubernatorial campaigns. She began at No Labels in 2009 and now serves as a senior advisor to the organization. Since beginning with No Labels, she has played an integral role in growing and developing the organization from an idea to a nationwide movement of more than half a million citizens. In her role, Margaret serves as a spokesperson and oversees all fundraising, congressional relations, and strategic execution of the staff, cofounders, executive board, and membership.

Margaret is a graduate of the University of South Carolina and is originally from North Carolina. She has returned to North Carolina where she now lives with her husband Matt and their dog.